Three Wise Men and a Baby

Three Wise Men and a Baby

David Robinson

MILTON KEYNES ● COLORADO SPRINGS ● HYDERABAD

13 12 11 10 09 08 07   7 6 5 4 3 2 1

First published 2007 by Authentic Media
9 Holdom Avenue, Bletchley, Milton Keynes, Bucks, MK1 1QR, UK
1820 Jet Stream Drive, Colorado Springs, CO 80921, USA
OM Authentic Media, Medchal Road, Jeedimetla Village, Secunderabad 500 055, A.P., India
www.authenticmedia.co.uk
Authentic Media is a division of IBS-STL U.K., limited by guarantee, with its Registered
Office at Kingstown Broadway, Carlisle, Cumbria CA3 0HA. Registered in England &
Wales No. 1216232. Registered charity 270162

British Library Cataloguing in Publication Data
A catalogue record for this book is available from the British Library

ISBN-13: 978-1-85078-789-1

Cover Design by fourninezero design.
Print Management by Adare Carwin
Printed and bound in Great Britain by William Clowes Ltd, Beccles, Suffolk

This book is dedicated to all Saltmine Theatre Company members
— past, present and future.

CONTENTS

ACKNOWLEDGEMENTS

The book-writing process can be a long journey and at times littered with delays. There are a number of people to whom I am very grateful.

My Saltmine family in Dudley.

My church family in Chesham.

My family family in Luton.

Also, for their patience, persuasion and persistence, Alison Hull, Jessica Turner and Sheila Jacobs . . . Three Wise Women and an Author.

PUBLIC PERFORMANCE

This book is a resource and you are free to use the material without a fee, although the author must be recognised in all publicity. Also, please keep Saltmine informed of any public performances of *Three Wise Men and a Baby*.

David

SETTING UP A DRAMA GROUP

Not too much is required in the formula for a successful drama group at your church. One is a bit of raw talent and two is a lot of preparation. For the ideal, and indeed, watchable result, my advice is not to compromise on either. Without the preparation and/or talent or experience, you would be well counselled not to allow a budding worship leader to be let loose on your opening hymn. The same is generally true for the majority of roles within the church setting, from the preacher downwards. Indeed, in one church I visited, I witnessed the joyful spectacle of someone being instructed in the locally accepted way of how to pass someone a hymn book on arrival at the church doors, whilst holding a fixed cheesy smile. Quite a performance. So, if someone tells you, as far as drama is concerned, you can just get up there and give it a go, can I ask you to be first to campaign for the abolition of such a process?

Audition

Alert people that you are searching for folk with a talent in acting, stage management and technical skills. And then meet them, talk to them and ask those with acting aspirations to try reading a prepared piece. To be professional and detailed at the start will only serve to help you when you get into the rehearsal schedule. Obviously you will need to treat the selection process carefully and sympathetically.

Try to use everyone who is attentive, but be realistic in what capacity you can use them. Take your time to consider who will be most suitable for lead roles, supporting roles, walk-on roles and the equally important backstage roles.

Preparation

There is no substitute for rehearsals. Never be under-rehearsed and don't be fooled into thinking you can be over-rehearsed. If you have the time, then keep rehearsing. Structure the rehearsal time, make it fun with sufficient time for feedback, discussion and refreshments. And always make sure you have done your homework if you are leading the rehearsal time. Set your goals, and be clear what you want to achieve during the rehearsal. As the performance date gets ever nearer, prepare for the extra rehearsals and always allow time for technical considerations.

Conclusion

Enthusiasm and fun are the key components to achieving success. Once you have found your relevant company members, add to their natural enthusiasm a healthy dose of commitment and push them to strive for professionalism and a strong team morale.

Any good acting company will need to support one another. They should be given the freedom to stretch one another artistically, to encourage one another and, above all, to feel comfortable to make mistakes in front of one another. You will have fun, you will make mistakes and, I can assure you, with each five-minute sketch, or with each one-hour production, you will improve.

Commend the actors, encourage the actors, criticise when you need to, and slowly − when the right people arrive − grow your team. And then, with each new piece you create you will see your budding troupe of actors not only improving but wanting to improve.

Enthusiasm − Fun − Commitment − Professionalism − Growth

DIRECTOR'S NOTES

The main note to accompany any production of *Three Wise Men and a Baby* is to have fun. Your resources may well dictate how adventurous or cautious you feel your production will be. The dialogue, of course, is your main thread, with the extra layers – songs, carols and dances – being interwoven in order to add to the festive feel. *Three Wise Men and a Baby* is about character, and the main note is to remember that with realism and truth will come the humour. Believe in your character, have sympathy with your character, and your audience will follow.

Try not to 'perform', try not to be comedic as yourself, just be your character and then allow Eric, Doreen, Brian and Marjorie to be as funny as they want to be. Indeed at times you'll need to allow them to be vulnerable. For them, it's in the dressing room and away from the lights (and Marjorie's constant stare) that the mask can come off. And the audience can be allowed in to share in a few private moments. One of the building blocks to your success with the production is to make sure you allow for the right balance of light and shade – the highs and the lows. From an all-singing, all-dancing 'Ding Dong Dance Routine' to a single-spot moment with a one-to-one between one of the characters and the audience, Eric, Doreen, Brian and Marjorie all need to be allowed to reveal their innermost fears and failings. Get the right emphasis between humour and pathos and you are well on the way to guaranteed success.

The other main players in the Christmas story are also profiled in the supporting sketches. If your numbers are limited with regards to performers, then you may find *One-Star Hotel* and the *Christmas Special* of some use to you at the appropriate Christmas event. And for a duologue, *And in that Same Field* takes an amusing glance at a couple of friendly, poetic shepherds.

Now, after what I'm sure will be the considerable success of your Christmas extravaganzas, no doubt approximately four months later your church leader will stride confidently up to you and ask the question, 'How about doing something dramatic for us over the Easter period?' Just in case that scenario comes true for you, I've included a couple of options: firstly, *Table for Thirteen*, an entertaining take on the Last Supper story through the eyes of the resident, and somewhat stressed, proprietor of the Pitchers of Water Restaurant and Conference Centre. And secondly, a rather more sober view on the Passion period with amazing early morning encounters as seen through the eyes of Judas, Mary and Simon Peter.

And so, finally, enjoy yourselves – and, in the words of Marjorie Lockwood, 'let's give it everything!'

THREE WISE MEN AND A BABY
An original Christmas play

David Robinson

CHARACTER NOTES

Brian Shepherd

'Lord, I'm here – Brian Shepherd, consultant accountant in the firm of Bayliss, Thorpe and Smith, church treasurer, lifelong fan of Preston North End, and a regular reserve for the Sunday prayer team.'

Of the scores of different characters I have played in my career, Brian Shepherd is my favourite. He's the nicest guy I know. I always feel a tremendous amount of warmth from the audience towards Brian – they have a genuine love for him.

I love playing Brian because he is completely different to me – I'm loud, he's quiet; I rush things yet he takes his time; I'm into skiing but he's into astronomy; I'm an actor and he's an accountant! But just thinking about him, there's more to it than that. I would be the life and soul of a party, the centre of attention, but Brian would be chatting to the person no one else noticed come in. I would say that I'll pray for someone then maybe do it every now and then when they came to mind, but Brian would set aside time each day to make sure he did. If nice guys finish last, then Brian would set a new world record for being in last place.

How Brian holds himself and moves is very important. I never try to make the early stages of Brian's movements too confident. A movement like getting up from a seat is a good example. I will generally start to get up and hesitate after a split second into the move and sit back quickly before then actually getting up. The whole move is over in the space of two seconds. Then why do it, you may ask. Well firstly, Brian, once he commits to something, will give it 100 per cent, whether that's a Michael Flatley 'Riverdance' impression in the 'Ding Dong Dance Routine' or a Christmas monologue for Ashleigh House Old People's home. But he will tend to question things before he does them even though he is likely to then go through with them anyway. Secondly, it's important to have little nuances and movements in your characterisation to create a more rounded character and to help you bond more with the part.

Some of the way that I play Brian was influenced by a character called David Stockwell from ITV1's drama *Heartbeat*. David is a very simple character; other characters are usually parental and essentially familial with him and, even though he gets things wrong, you can't help but like him. This is very similar to Brian; obviously, as an accountant, Brian is far more intelligent than David is, but it's important to remember that intelligent people are not always intellectual. Doreen is very maternal towards Brian; she worries about whether he is happy and also tries to match-make for him. And both Eric and Doreen were unaware of Brian losing his mother to cancer even though they've known him four years. If you can watch any *Heartbeat* episodes with David in it, David Lonsdale's performance is a joy to watch.

All that remains to say is, enjoy every second of playing this part; having performed as Brian over seventy-five times I can say that I'm really going to miss him.

Michael Taylor

Doreen Wiseman

After performing the character of Doreen for several tours, this is my concept for her character. However, it is only my opinion and your own interpretation would be far more beneficial to you – and I'm sure you would enjoy it more because it will give you a greater sense of ownership over the character.

First, let us begin with fact. Doreen is the middle child with two sisters, both of whom are very successful. She doesn't believe she has any particular gifting: 'Not like Debs or Denise, anyway.' She confesses to feeling 'trapped in the middle', both in family life and between Eric and the church, so there is a lot of underlying frustration. She feels like she's failing her parents who don't approve of Eric (they expected her to marry a doctor or a vet or something), nor are they proud of her (particularly when her mother comments continually on the state of their house), although we find out later that her family prefer to spend their Christmases with her because it is a nice atmosphere. She has a gift of hospitality.

Doreen is a vicar's wife, the vicar being the Reverend Eric Wiseman, and so is very involved with church groups like the St Mary's Literary Society and the Mother's Union. A lot of what she says is information she is relaying to Eric. So she appears very organised and seems to know exactly what is going on with everyone. Eric admires her and sees her as a pragmatist – 'feet on the ground, nothing fancy'. She cares about people and expresses her desire to 'be there' for people, to learn to love and serve and forgive those around her. She's compassionate and encouraging and particularly cares for Brian, inviting him to stay every Christmas, giving him sound advice and continually trying to set him up with Betty Bouston (apparently she's been plotting for years).

Character quirks are that she's afraid of camels due to an experience on the banks of the Read Sea where one spat in her face; consequently, Omar the camel makes her anxious and annoyed. She also doesn't like too much sun as it brings her out in a rash. She has a dry, sarcastic sense of humour that stems from her matter-of-factness. She is conscious of her appearance; not eating too many biscuits before Christmas and thinking about getting her 'colours done'. She struggles to forgive people like Mrs Viney who comment on her open-toed sandals.

She worries about what other people are thinking but wishes she didn't – maybe this is why she doesn't always tell people about her Christian activities.

Miriam Sarin

Eric Wiseman

I remember when David Robinson first wrote *Three Wise Men and a Baby* and presented it to Saltmine Theatre Company, telling me that he had me in mind for the role of Eric. I had an odd feeling reading the play, particularly my part, a feeling of 'Oh, so this is how you see me!' This was paranoia of course, but the feeling wouldn't go. More terrifying was the horrible feeling that he might have been right.

Eric is a vicar. We know (or at least Doreen thinks) that he works really hard at this job. However, we also know (because he tells us) that he is worried about the state of his faith. He compares it to the prop gold that is used in the *We Three Sing* musical – a shoe box wrapped in gold paper, hollow. He is a performer. He acts in the play, he says (in the long monologue at the end of Act 1) that he desired fame and he describes his duties as a vicar as like elements of performance ('I know my lines, most of my moves').

To be honest, I could relate to this. I'm not a vicar, I'm an actor, an actor who has spent the best part of his career in Christian theatre and worked really hard at it. But have I worked so hard at my job, so hard at talking about my faith through performance that the faith itself has shrivelled and become an empty shell? I hope not, but I think it's a constant danger.

Different actors have different approaches. Some try to get the character's walk or work out their costume. I try to imaginatively connect with my character, with their emotions. I ask how I would feel in their situation. In this case I was able to use my own feelings of insecurity and doubt and filter them through the character.

Once the internal feelings were in place I found that the externals came very easily. It seemed to me that Eric has incredible amounts of energy onstage and is nearly always tired when he isn't performing. I found that my body wanted to slouch as Eric and that he tends to slightly shuffle his feet when he walks.

In a sense, although Eric didn't sound like me or walk like me, ultimately I think my performance was really about who I am, and what I fear.

All of which sounds like quite heavy preparation for what is, after all, a comedy! Nevertheless, I do think that it lies at the heart of Eric's character. He jokes, he does his very best in the play, he works hard for the church; maybe it's because he knows that if he stops, he'll have to face questions that it's easier to ignore.

This is not to deny that as an actor you can have a whale of a time doing your best bad Shakespearean acting (think Olivier meets Kenneth Williams), cheesy American game show host and crooner!

Ultimately though, his journey in the play is to get to a point where he realises that he has to stop. In other words, by the end of the play he has reached a point where his real journey can begin. I hope that other people can enjoy playing Eric as much as I have.

Richard Hasnip

Marjorie Lockwood

I hope I'm right in saying that this part was not written 'for me' as I don't think anyone would readily admit to being a Marjorie. Don't get me wrong; she's great fun to play, but she is not someone that you would warm to easily.

What first stuck me was that Marjorie has very little dialogue with the other characters. By that I mean, it's not very conversational; she comes on and talks at the other characters, then leaves. She is the leader everyone loves to hate, or rather, loves to complain about. She is bossy and demanding and not very sensitive. She thoroughly believes in what she's doing but has slight delusions of grandeur, believing that St Mary's Literacy Society's production of *We Three Sing* could be what puts her on the map as a nationally respected director. She would never admit as much but why else would she start rehearsals for a Christmas show in August? She is a perfectionist yet seems to have quite bad taste in terms of what is suitable for a family friendly am dram Christmas play (belly dancing and live camels for example). She is brave and ambitious and doesn't believe that anything is impossible.

When exploring how to play Marjorie, I found myself being influenced by comedians like Julie Walters and Victoria Wood, especially in regards to her voice, body language and use of funny costumes and hats. I decided that Marjorie would be the type to try and dress the part of director (emphasis on try). Her clothes would get more and more flamboyant and ridiculous as the play progresses, and always with a different hat or headgear of some sort (antlers and flashing nose during the singing of 'Rudolph the Red-Nosed Reindeer' for example). This is particularly effective since she often appears for very short times adding a comic visual punch-line to some scenes. The key with Marjorie is to make the most of her; she's often not in a scene for long so you have to communicate as much as you can in that short moment. There's no such thing as being too over the top with Marjorie. Everything she says and does is big and loud, but what adds to the humour is that she takes herself extremely seriously.

There is a deeper side to her, though, which doesn't get seen much, but if captured, will make her a far more believable person and less of a comic caricature.

In her monologue we realise that Marjorie's life is far less glamorous than she may have you believe. She may dream of stardom and the spotlight but when the show's over the reality is she works in a bakery. When she's not got her head in the clouds directing, her life is ordinary and humdrum. St Mary's Literary Society is an escape from that fact. For those few months she is important, she has a role, she is in charge and she may even get a mention in the local paper! The really sad thing is that she's lonely. She knows a lot of people but they are what I'd call acquaintances rather then friends. This is highlighted by the fact that we never see her having a meaningful conversation with any of the other characters in the play. She is totally engrossed in the play and shows little interest in the actors' personal lives. Putting up a professional front in rehearsals is an effective way of masking the fact that she has little or no relationship with the rest of the cast. She alludes to this in her monologue, describing parties as having 'all sorts of people I don't really know'. Pride, I believe, prevents her from rectifying this.

Katharine Henthorne

CAST

Brian Shepherd

Doreen Wiseman

Eric Wiseman

Marjorie Lockwood

Eric covers the role of Marco Bellini

Doreen covers the role of Vanessa

Fingers Freddie

NOTE: If you struggle to find a stage manager (SM) or someone to do the live voice offs (V/O), it would be quite acceptable for Marjorie to be the voice.

PROPS

<u>IN DRESSING ROOM AREA/PERFORMANCE AREA</u>

Hamper

Table

2 chairs

Mirror

Make-up box

Rail with stage costumes

Kettle, 2 mugs

Shoe box – gold

Glass bottle – frankincense

Ornament – myrrh

Pocket Bible

Christian devotions

2 horses' heads on sticks

Rudolf's red nose

Agatha Christie novel, flyer/programme for show

1 pantomime camel

Pin the Tail on the Ox (hardboard with detachable tail)

<u>VICARAGE LOUNGE</u>

Christmas cards

2 chairs

Coffee table

Christmas tree

Decorations

Bookcase

Diary

Newspaper

2 mugs

Biscuits on a tray

Christmas presents - wrapped

<u>FOR ORCHESTRA PIT</u>

Large Christmas tree

Keyboard with mic

Boom mic stand

Straight mic stand (1950s style mic)

Hand-held mic for Eric as Marco Bellini

ACT 1

*Starts in blackout. We hear the carol 'As With
Gladness Men of Old' being sung – slow fade up of
spotlight to reveal Eric, Doreen and Brian singing the
first verse. The first verse ends, the singers remain
transfixed, spotlight up on Marjorie (downstage left)
sat on a director's chair facing the stage.*

Marjorie: Lovely, thanks everyone. Doreen, sweetie,
you're still in a key all of your own,
darling – and not one I recognise. Nor, I
suspect, will anyone else! Now, there's no
rehearsal next Monday as it's a bank
holiday, so the next rehearsal is Monday the
sixth at 7.30 sharp. Now, can we have books
down by then, everyone, it will only be
fifteen weeks to curtain up. Brian, love,
any news on the camel? I'm not fussed about
it being a dromedary. But I could do with
knowing well before the dress. And can
someone tell Eileen that as well as being

prompter she'll have to stand by with
sawdust and a bucket every night in the
wings. All right, everyone, have a good
break – and remember, wise men, keep
practising the funny walk – think camel
everyone. Thanks everyone, and remember,
it'll soon be Christmas!

Blackout. Music for 'Little Donkey' in the blackout.
Lights up on the vicarage dressed for Christmas. Eric
is bringing in coffee for himself and his wife
Doreen, who is sitting at the coffee table writing
Christmas cards.

ERIC: One hump or two?

DOREEN: I beg your pardon?

ERIC: Sorry, lump, not hump. I'm thinking camel at
            all times, as per instructions.

DOREEN: Just one – and no biscuits. I always feel
            better over Christmas if I've gone easy on
            the biscuits during the previous fortnight.
            False economy, I know. Thanks, love. *(pause)*
            Is she still serious about that camel?

ERIC: I've got no idea. She was in one of her
            Spielberg moods last night: 'Please
            everyone, no questions, I need space to
            create.'

DOREEN: Well, I can tell you this now, Eric. I am
            not going anywhere near a camel. I still
            come out in a rash whenever I think of that
            one that spat at me on the banks of the Red
            Sea.

ERIC: We are two of the wise men, love. We arrive
            on the thing. Act Two Scene Three, halfway

down page seventeen. Of course you'll have
to go near it!

DOREEN: Where does she intend to keep the thing?
            It's a camel for goodness' sake, not a
            gerbil.

ERIC: In the Boy's Brigade cupboard, last time I
            heard. I shouldn't worry - she won't go
            through with it. I mean, you remember last
            year and Mrs Grainger's Alsatian? It still
            hasn't recovered from its role in the
            'Little Donkey Dance Routine'. It walks with
            a limp and growls whenever Suzie in her
            Virgin Mary outfit comes anywhere near it.

DOREEN: Well, I think that'll do for now. Just
            remember we've stopped at Auntie Mavis'
            card. All right?

Eric is scanning the local paper.

DOREEN: Any mention of the spectacular in the local
            rag?

ERIC: *(reading)* 'St Mary's Literary Society will
            be presenting their latest seasonal treat,
            the musical *We Three Sing*, based rather
            loosely on the traditional story of the
            three wise men. Director Marjorie Lockwood
            says the evening promises to be a magical
            treat following the three wise men on their
            journey amongst the stars! Miss Lockwood has
            even hinted about the appearance of a real-
            life camel. The cast is led by Reverend Eric
            Wiseman, his wife Doreen and church
            treasurer Brian Shepherd as the three kings.
            The show opens next Friday at the St Mary's
            church hall at 7.30pm and finishes Saturday
            at 3pm with a matinee. Tickets are available

from the church office. Come and discover what the wise men were really searching for.'

Music – 'We Three Kings of Orient Are'.

BRIAN (as NARRATOR): *(assertively)* When Jesus was born in the village of Bethlehem in Judea, Harold was king.

MARJORIE: Herod!

BRIAN: Herod was king. During this time, some wise men from the east came to Jerusalem and said, 'Where is the child born to be king of the... ' *(dries)*

MARJORIE: *(whispering)* King of the Jews *(louder)*, King of the Jews!

BRIAN: *(mimicking Marjorie)* King of the Jews! We saw his star and have come to worship him.

MARJORIE: Lovely, Brian, remember your diction. Now, straight into Herod with the chief priests. Think pace everyone. Don't forget you're the baddies; we want the audience really booing at this stage.

DOREEN: Don't worry, they will be!

Eric/Herod enters walking with a limp and humped back, he is hamming the role. He is followed by two chief priests – Brian and Doreen.

HEROD: *(rather angry)* I'm telling you there were three of them, three kings surrounding me. It was like having a conversation with a pack of cards.

PRIEST ONE/DOREEN: These are eastern kings you speak of, Your Majesty. Placed in such a lofty position through wisdom and their stargazing.

PRIEST TWO/BRIAN: We know of only one great king, Your Majesty.

HEROD: Then why did they speak of this King of the Jews? They wanted to worship him, not me. They called him the Messiah.

PRIEST ONE: Did they?

PRIEST TWO: An interesting name. Not sure what it means – are you?

HEROD: Never mind interesting. I want to know where this Messiah is to be born.

PRIEST TWO: The prophets tell us that he is to be born in Bethlehem, Your Messiah. *(nudged by Doreen)* Majesty!

HEROD: Bethlehem, really. Well, let's have another word with these so-called wise men, shall we? Let's get them to lead us directly to this wonderful King of the Jews. *(baddie laughter from all three. Brian and Doreen exit leaving Herod laughing on his own. He notices then exits)*

MARJORIE: *(back in director's chair)* Very nice everyone, thanks. Eric *(Eric, Doreen and Brian re-enter)*, I think my note about basing it around Richard the Third has probably pushed you slightly over the top. Can we drop the limp, love? By the way, Bristol Zoo has agreed to open up discussions on a camel, everyone. He's a ten-year-old double hump called Omar, and

apparently has no objections to wearing a
fez. Now I would like to do the 'Wise men in
your own words' exercise I talked about. I
trust you are all prepared. Can we start
with Casper, please – that's right, you,
Brian, love. I want to hear about
similarities between yourself and your
character.

*Blackout. Lights up on the dressing room. Brian is
sitting by the dresser.*

BRIAN: *(talks to audience, slowly)* I'm thinking that
            Casper is about forty, forty-one. I'm only
            thirty, so that's not really much of a
            similarity. Except, I suppose Casper was
            thirty once, about ten years ago I expect.
            I think he's probably married – but goes away
            a lot with the other two perhaps – the wise
            men, I mean – or... or maybe on his own. Like
            me, really. Well no, I mean, I'm not married,
            but I do go away quite a bit, mostly on my
            own. I like to travel – visit, like the wise
            men. Not on a camel though.
            I prefer walking by myself – the Lake
            District or the Peaks. Yorkshire Dales last
            year. Casper goes away at Christmas –
            following the star, searching for something.
            I always go away at Christmas; not quite sure
            if I'm searching for something, but I always
            get away, well, last five or six years or so
            at least. People always ask me to join them
            for Christmas, you know, round here – Eric
            and Doreen, Bill and Ivy, Joanne Levvy.
            I tell them thanks, but I'd rather not. It's
            a family time really, isn't it? You know,
            couples and kids and the like. It would be
            different, I suppose, if I were marr... but
            I'm not. So I say no thanks. And I get away.

Went to the top of Scotland last year, it
was a wonderful experience. Saw the Northern
Lights – amazing really, Christmas Eve it
was, and the Aurora Borealis lighting up the
blackened sky. It seemed just then that it
was doing it just for me, you know.
I couldn't see another soul; no one, just
me. It felt like a very reassuring moment
for me. I've brought it to mind quite a bit
this year. You know, when I've felt a bit
low, bit lonely at times, I suppose. I mean,
nothing compared to what Casper had to think
back on. I mean, I don't think I could
afford to bring any expensive aromatic oils
to him like Casper was able to do. But, you
know, when I stood in front of those
Northern Lights, I was able to say to him
again: Lord, I'm here – Brian Shepherd,
consultant accountant in the firm of
Bayliss, Thorpe and Smith, church treasurer,
lifelong fan of Preston North End and a
regular reserve for the Sunday prayer team.
I think Casper got to Bethlehem and found
what he was searching for. I get the feeling
I'm still looking – but I'm here, Lord...
I've got my gifts for you... such as they
are... still searching, Lord... *(breaks off,
slow lights fade)* Still searching.
(blackout)

*Lights up on the vicarage. Music – 'Rocking Around
the Christmas Tree'. Eric is dealing with decorations,
Doreen is wrapping a present.*

DOREEN: There's lavender bath salts for your Aunt
          Irene, and a spotted tie for your Uncle
          Bill. Again.

ERIC: They will be surprised.

DOREEN: I'm not sure surprise comes into it. They've
          bought us place mats for the last fourteen
          years. Goodness knows how long they think
          our dining table is.

ERIC: You know, I've yet to see Uncle Bill wear
          any of the ties we've bought him.

DOREEN: *(picking up a hideous tie)* Can you blame
          him?

ERIC: They will probably look out for the place
          mats on Boxing Day during the buffet.

DOREEN: I always use 'London Landmarks' and
          'Constable Country'. The others are hideous.

ERIC: Yes, surprisingly the 'Benidorm by Night'
          set rarely makes an appearance.

DOREEN: No, nor curiously does the rather risqué
          'Farmyard Animals at Springtime' ever
          venture out of the bottom sideboard drawer.

ERIC: Boxing Day!! Now, there's a wonderful
          thought. Could we just cut straight to it,
          do you think?

DOREEN: We've got two performances of the panto
          extravaganza to get through before that, as
          well as three mince pie parties, the Festive
          Bazaar, Christmas Eve Communion, Christmas
          Day sermon followed by a lunchtime trip to
          Ashleigh Nursing Home in a Santa outfit. And
          then finally we can look forward to a Boxing
          Day with family, friends and that strange
          cousin of yours from Blackburn.

ERIC: Have we asked Brian?

DOREEN: He declined of course. Said thanks but he's
          booked a trip to the Orkneys, should be back
          for New Year.

ERIC: I do worry about him sometimes, you know.
          Is he happy, do you think?

DOREEN: At times yes, very happy; think of the
          rehearsal last week. He was in hysterics.

ERIC: Everyone was in hysterics by the end of it.
          Apart from Marjorie, of course.

SM: *(V/O on tannoy)* 'Ding Dong Dance Routine' –
          places on stage everyone!

*Music from 'Ding Dong Merrily on High'. There then
follows 'The Ding Dong Dance Routine'. Eric, Doreen
and Brian make a desperately poor yet funny attempt
at it; in some of the improvisation Brian attempts
'Riverdance'; it ends in blackout.*

*Lights up on Brian in his dressing room, checking his
lines. Eric enters with two coffees.*

ERIC: Coffee, Brian?

BRIAN: Yes, thanks... if there's nothing stronger?

ERIC: Surely not. Church coffee and strength
          seldom go together in my experience. How are
          the lines coming on?

BRIAN: About as quickly as the dance steps at the
          moment. I mean, we open in two days, Eric.
          Last run through, I arrived at the manger
          without my myrrh, for goodness' sake.

ERIC: He probably didn't need it... never sure
          what it is anyway.

BRIAN: Never fear. Marjorie slipped me a definition
          during week eleven of rehearsals. It's the
          aromatic resin obtained from several
          burseraceous trees and shrubs of Africa and
          South Asia.

ERIC: No newborn baby should be without it! You'll
          be fine, Brian, I promise. You do know it,
          you know; we've had books down since August
          bank holiday. It's just nerves getting the
          better of you, I promise. Besides, we've all
          got nervous recently. Doreen turns a funny
          colour at the mere mention of Omar the
          camel. It's just the opening night seems a
          lot closer, that's all.

BRIAN: Is he joining us?

ERIC: Who?

BRIAN: Omar the camel.

ERIC: Marjorie is taking an urgent call from
          Bristol Zoo as we speak and 'can't possibly
          be disturbed for twenty minutes at least'.

BRIAN: Why on earth I agreed to do this I shall
          never know. I don't know, I really don't
          know.

ERIC: Because I suspect somebody asked you to do
          it, and when someone asks you sweetly, you
          generally oblige. That's you, Brian. And
          it's a great quality - but can result in you
          arriving in a place you don't really want to
          be in.

BRIAN: Like this dressing room, for instance.

ERIC: Probably yes. But listen, at the end of the
          day, this is St Mary's Literary Society

doing their best for two shows to a hundred people at the most. A hundred people who will love it whatever befalls you, me, Doreen and Omar the camel. They will look at you and say, 'Good on you, Brian, entertaining the kids, not afraid to make a fool of yourself, raising money for charity, remembering all your lines and mastering the quick step to boot.' Believe me, you will be OK, Brian... Just wish you could enjoy it. *(pause)* You don't want it spoiling your Christmas, now, do you? You've got your holiday to look forward to.

BRIAN: *(pause)* No. No, I suppose not.

ERIC: The Orkneys, isn't it? Doreen mentioned it.

BRIAN: Yes, yes that's right. I go on the twenty-third. Should be back for New Year.

ERIC: Weren't you up there last year?

BRIAN: *(a little uncomfortable)* No. I was on the mainland last year. Little hotel just outside Wick. Beautiful headland just nearby. Where I saw the lights, of course.

ERIC: Christmas lights?

BRIAN: Northern Lights. Just me out on the cliffs, late on Christmas Eve and suddenly the sky was doing a light show for me with the stars. It was a very special night for me, Eric. I'd gone up there full of doubt and worries and, I'm sorry to say, a pretty delicate faith. But, you know, just at that moment it was... it was restored for me, mended if you like. He hadn't forgotten me.

ERIC: Sounds wonderful.

BRIAN: It was. And... and I want to see it again...
           you know, the lights. Just to... to remind
           myself again of his power, his majesty, his
           restoration, his forgiveness... er, yes.

ERIC: Forgiveness? What for?

Doreen bursts in.

DOREEN: We're needed on stage now. Marjorie wants to
           see Herod and his cronies part two – and
           Eric, she says bring back Richard the Third,
           we're low on laughs in the third scene.

Eric is getting into his Herod garb.

ERIC: Any news on Omar?

DOREEN: We need to be checked out by a vet,
           apparently.

ERIC: He's not taking my temperature, I can assure
           you.

MARJORIE: *(rushing on)* Places, everyone!

*Loud crash of thunder, sinister lights. Eric acts out
the monologue with actions for the lines; he is
hamming again.*

ERIC: *(as Richard the Third)* Now is the winter of our
           discontent
           Made glorious summer by this son of York;
           And all the clouds that lour'd upon our
           house
           In the deep bosom of the ocean buried.
           Now are our brows bound with victorious
           wreaths;
           Our bruised arms hung up for monuments;

Our stern alarums changed to merry meetings,
Our dreadful marches to delightful measures.
Grim-visaged war hath smooth'd his wrinkled
front;
And now, instead of mounting barded steeds
To fright the souls of fearful adversaries,
He capers nimbly in a lady's chamber
To the lascivious pleasing of a lute.
But I, that am not shaped for sportive
tricks,
Nor made to court an amorous looking-glass;
I, that am rudely stamp'd, and want love's
majesty
To strut before a wanton ambling nymph;
I, that am curtail'd of this fair
proportion,
Cheated of feature by dissembling nature,
Deformed, unfinish'd, sent before my time
Into this breathing world, scarce half made
up,
And that so lamely and unfashionable
That dogs bark at me as I halt by them;
Why, I, in this weak piping time of peace,
Have no delight to pass away the time,
Unless to spy my shadow in the sun
And descant on mine own deformity
And therefore, since I cannot prove a lover,
To entertain these fair well-spoken days,
I am determined to prove a villain.

MARJORIE: *(comes to join him)* That's lovely, darling!
I'm not quite sure what it means but I'm
sure they'll love it – and don't forget that
while you're doing that, Betty Bouston and
her troupe will be doing a tap dance around
you. But don't be put off by that.

*Eric reacts as blackout. Lights come up on the
dressing room.*

DOREEN: *(to audience)* I suspect Balthazar was a man,
           for starters. It's always been the three
           wise *men* as far as I can remember. Balthazar
           is the one in the middle – I see him in
           light blue with a flowing cloak and a sort
           of turban on his head, with possibly a huge
           gold medallion showing off his Mediterranean
           tan. Dark set eyes, deep voice and a rather
           cheeky sense of humour. Quite like the sound
           of him, actually. Not sure where our
           similarities are, to be honest. I always
           think I look slightly better in darker
           colours. I did wonder about having my
           colours done. You know, find out if I'm a
           summer or an autumn or whatever. Eric thinks
           it's a waste of time – 'You dress *for* a
           season, not *in* a season' is his set
           response. He likes his set responses does
           Eric, he has one for most occasions. A very
           annoying habit. He's probably right though,
           he usually is. That's another annoying habit
           he's acquired.

           I don't know about similarities – but I can
           think of a distinct difference. I suspect
           Balthazar is happy with both camels and hot
           weather. I'm not so good with either. Eric
           persuaded me to help him lead a church trip
           to the Holy Land a few years ago when we
           were at our last parish. Two things are
           guaranteed to bring me out in a prickly rash
           – one is too much exposure to the sun, and
           the other is the thought of that vicious
           camel on the banks of the Red Sea. The
           imminent arrival of Omar in a Tommy Cooper
           fez is doing nothing for my nerves, let
           alone my skin tone. Being in the middle
           (pause), I can certainly relate to that. I'm
           number two of three daughters. Deborah's the
           eldest and Denise is five years younger than

me. Denise had done brilliantly, studied
law, married a fellow student and they both
work for a top-notch firm in the city.
Deborah has done equally well. She went to
work for an estate agent straight from
school. She's now a partner responsible for
six shops - she has a stunning husband
called Clive, three kids and a German
Shepherd, a heated swimming pool, a tennis
court and a cottage in Norfolk.

(pause) Do you know what they've both got?
They've got parents who are very proud of
what they've achieved. Not sure I've got
that. Not yet anyway. And unless Eric is in
line for the old purple shirt and funny hat,
I'm not sure I ever will. Mother always saw
me marrying a doctor or a vet. Oh, I know
they love me...and they tolerate Eric. Mum
doesn't have to say anything, I just know
what she's thinking. Particularly when they
come to stay at the vicarage for the
weekend. The inconsistent heating, the
dribbly shower, the lack of nets, the need
for a new rug in the lounge, and that odd
stain on the floor in the bathroom. Dad just
slumps down in the sofa on Sunday afternoon,
and gently falls asleep with quiet mumblings
about us not having Sky Sports.

I feel a bit trapped in the middle, you
know. I just want to please Mum and Dad, I
want them to be really proud of me and Eric.
He does a good job, he really does. And I do
my very best to help him. To be there. To...
not be in the way, but to be there. I'm in
the middle here as well sometimes, I feel I
get between Eric and the church somehow. You
know, occasionally I think he'd move his bed
into that vestry if he had the chance - he

lives for that place, he works so hard.
Clive was very good - Deb's husband. He took
us for a ride in his new Volvo. Sometimes he
said, maybe you need to look at it the other
way around. Maybe it's the church that's
coming between you and Eric, not you coming
between the Eric and the church.

So there was Balthazar on 'camel number
two', no pink rash and a tan to die for.
He was probably being led by camel number
one and concerned that Casper on camel
number three was moaning about him. But he
was there with his gift, and his desire to
search.

I don't know about having any sort of gift.
Not like Debs or Denise, anyway. But I want
to find a time when I can not worry about
what others are thinking. When I can really
serve others and love them, warts and all.
To be there for Eric, for Mum, Dad and the
family. And to really love and learn to
forgive those around me - particularly in
church. And particularly Mrs Viney and her
comments about my open-toed sandals and lack
of hat, during Communion.

I know it's somewhere - God. Somewhere.
Still searching for now. I'm still
searching.

Fade to blackout. Music - 'O Little Town of Bethlehem'.

MARJORIE: *(as Eric, Doreen and stage manager are
randomly on stage 'checking' spots, lights
and going through the dance)* All right,
everyone, it's final dress rehearsal with
full technical additions as well. So prepare
yourself for a long evening. We've got tea,

coffee, ham sandwiches and paracetamols in
the small kitchen, Babs wants to check make-
up and costume, Di's on props, and make sure
you mark all your dramatic pauses in
Eileen's prompter script. We're still
waiting for the Health and Safety clearance
with regards to Omar's cage. So, wise men,
be prepared for an alternative on opening
night tomorrow. Now, nobody rush off at the
end – I still want to do one or two cuts.
I'm still thinking three and three-quarter
hours is a little on the long side for the
kiddies. Not to mention the OAPs' matinee,
and Mr Barker's snoring. But can we just
hold going in to the next scene. I've got
Health and Safety waiting for me in the
Mother's Union room. Take five everyone.

Marjorie exits.

ERIC: I've never found the Mother's Union
           particularly good for my health or my
           safety.

DOREEN: Speaking of the Mother's Union, Mrs Myatt
           brought some mince pies round for you.
           She said to remind you that the Christmas
           special is on Tuesday. They've given you an
           extra five minutes, but could you please be
           finished prompt at twenty past, so Mrs
           Prendergast can remind everyone what they
           can do with their unwanted poinsettias.

ERIC: I could give them one or two suggestions.

DOREEN: They want your talk title by 6.30 this
           evening, together with your Bible reference.
           Any idea what you're going to talk about yet
           at the Mother's Union?

Brian enters upstage.

ERIC: But of course I know exactly what I'm going
           to say to the Mother's Union! Philippians
           chapter 2 verses 12 to 16. *(Eric refers to
           his pocket Bible)* 'Do everything without
           complaining or arguing, so that you may become
           blameless and pure, children of God without
           fault in a crooked and depraved generation, in
           which you shine like stars in the universe as
           you hold out the word of life - in order that
           I may boast on the day of Christ that I did
           not run or labour for nothing.'

BRIAN: One of my favourite passages.

ERIC: Then I want to talk to them about us,
           actually.

BRIAN: Us?

ERIC: Well, not exactly us. I mean us three.
           The wise men. I was going to start by
           getting them all to give me their birthday
           dates and read them their stars from the
           Mail on Sunday.

DOREEN: Read their stars, Eric! You can't possibly
           do that. You'll be up before the Bishop
           before Christmas, explaining yourself.

BRIAN: You'll be up before Mrs Myatt, which has got
           to be significantly more worrying!

ERIC: Well, it's stargazing. I think people get
           our wonderful characters mixed up. You know,
           astrologers, astronauts. I'm never quite
           sure about the distinction.

BRIAN: Astrology is the once supposed science
           looking at the influence of stars on human

and terrestrial affairs. Astronomy is the
science of heavenly bodies.

ERIC: The science of heavenly bodies. Rather
            appropriate for the Mother's Union.

BRIAN: So I think that makes us astrologers,
            not astronomers.

ERIC: Us?

BRIAN: The three wise men.

ERIC: Yes. Yes, of course. Listen, Brian, why don't
            you take your life in your hands and come
            with me to the Christmas Mother's Union. You
            could share your Northern Lights experience.

DOREEN: What was that, Brian?

BRIAN: It was... nothing really. Just a...

ERIC: Listen, you tell Doreen. If Doreen is
            entertained, the Mother's Union will be no
            problem. *(Doreen glares at Eric)* I'll make
            some coffee. *(exit Eric)*

BRIAN: I feel as though I'm being cornered here.
            Eric told you the Northern Lights story,
            didn't he?

DOREEN: Sounds wonderful. I had no idea you were
            interested in the stars, Brian.

BRIAN: I wasn't really, till last year. Now I'm
            surrounded by books and magazines, videos,
            the lot. I treated myself to a telescope in
            the summer. Let me know when I'm boring you.

DOREEN: It can't be boring, Brian. Eric couldn't
            wait to tell me all about your experience
            when he got home. That's what he means about

giving a talk; it's not necessarily the subject that makes people listen – it's your enthusiasm for it. You know, Brian, I think you're a very positive person at heart. Listen, I know you don't always think you show it, but for me and Eric, you're good company; you give us hope, and optimism.

BRIAN: You can't support Preston North End and not give out optimism. I appreciate what you've said. And your concern, both of you.

DOREEN: Eric was worried he'd upset you the other day. You know, in the dressing room.

BRIAN: No, no he didn't.

DOREEN: It's just that he said you got a bit... well, you went quiet, talked about waiting to be forgiven? Or something.

BRIAN: Yes. Yes, I'm sorry about that. Just had a few difficult memories, don't know why they came to me just then.

DOREEN: It's nothing new. Christmas is a time for memories for lots of people. It can be a difficult time for a great many folk, Brian. It's not something you should punish yourself over.

BRIAN: I don't think I realised I had until last year.

DOREEN: It must have been quite an enlightening moment.

BRIAN: In many ways. (*pause*) Have you heard of Polaris, Doreen?

DOREEN: I think I may have done. Not sure.

BRIAN: It's also known as the Pole Star or the
            North Star.

DOREEN: Right, yes, OK. You know stars aren't my
            strong point. Apart from the celebrity type,
            of course. Don't tell Mrs Myatt but I get *OK*
            magazine on a regular basis.

BRIAN: I was reading up on the North Star last year
            when I was away. The dictionary definition
            is 'a star very near the north pole of the
            heavens'.

DOREEN: Sounds like quite a special star.

BRIAN: It is, it is. Like the one that led the wise
            men. *(pause)*

DOREEN: What is it, Brian? What's holding you back?

BRIAN: Do you believe in heaven, Doreen? I mean,
            really believe?

DOREEN: Yes, yes I do... I have a real hope for
            heaven. I'm not in a desperate rush to see
            it, but yes, I believe in it.

BRIAN: That's good.

DOREEN: But I'm under no illusion that it's not an
            easy concept. A vast vault of sky, the
            dwelling place of God, a place of blissful
            happiness, with angels and harps and
            whatever. Not an easy place to picture.

BRIAN: It's a real place, do you think?

DOREEN: Not with pearly gates and a big front door,
            I don't think so, no. But yes, it's real,
            it's a place of peace and joy and being with
            God – and nothing getting in the way. *(pause)*

BRIAN: I always have to think back to my mother
            dying, you see.

DOREEN: Go on, Brian.

BRIAN: It was a couple of years before you got
            here; she was only in her sixties.

DOREEN: I'm sorry... you never mentioned...

BRIAN: She contracted cancer, went downhill very
            quickly. We only had each other as far as
            family goes. She was in dreadful pain day
            and night and wanted to go to 'that better
            place' as soon as she could.

DOREEN: She believed in heaven?

BRIAN: She did. I didn't. To me, leaving me didn't
            mean going to a better place. I couldn't
            tell her... I wanted to but I couldn't tell
            her that I thought she was going to a better
            place. I was bitter with God and wanted her
            to stay here with me. To me, this was the
            better place.

DOREEN: So you thought.

BRIAN: Yes. And you see, I've never forgiven myself
            for that. Never.

DOREEN: Brian, I don't think its your own forgiveness
            you're searching for. What you felt was only
            natural. You loved your mum and you wanted
            to stay together. She knew she wanted freedom
            from the pain and suffering, and knew she
            could head for a better place. She's there
            now, Brian, free of pain and suffering, and
            sitting amongst the stars.

BRIAN: I hope so.

DOREEN: It's not something you can see through a
            telescope, Brian.

BRIAN: Knowing Mum she'll be sat on the North Star,
            close to all the action.

DOREEN: Why did you, er, choose the section in
            Philippians as a favourite?

BRIAN: Shining like the stars? Something I want to
            do one day.

DOREEN: Quite a possibility. You know, Brian, you'll
            never be a frontline person; you don't grab
            the limelight, or seek stardom.

BRIAN: Wise man number *three*, that's me.

DOREEN: Exactly, but you shine for God, more than
            most people I've ever known. And that
            includes the vicar. That's why he wants you
            to talk to Mrs Myatt and the gang. Not to
            give them a lecture on astronomy but to tell
            them about you. What you do to please God
            and other people – you always have done ever
            since I've known you. That's why you agreed
            to do the third wise man on the left for
            Marjorie Lockwood. That's why you're the
            treasurer, and a steward, and on the prayer
            team, and a hundred other things. You don't
            need to ask God or your mum or anyone for
            forgiveness, I think the Northern Lights told
            you that, didn't they? A special light show,
            just for you. That's what you told Eric.

BRIAN: The Aurora Borealis.

DOREEN: Exactly. You know, there's another verse
            that's a favourite of mine, that's applicable
            to you. Daniel chapter 12 verse 3.

BRIAN: Go on.

DOREEN: 'Everyone who has been wise' (or has been a
            'wise man') 'will shine as bright as the sky
            above, and everyone who has led others to
            please God will shine like the stars.' You're
            pleasing God, Brian, as well as your mum.

Music – 'Silent Night' as they hug and lights fade.

MARJORIE: *(standing on platform speaking out to
            audience)* All right, everyone. I've got
            notes for you all. Particularly you, Eric,
            your concentration is all over the place.
            Can you try not to dump the block of gold on
            Joseph's foot? I don't want laughs at that
            moment. All right, Eric, love, are you still
            OK to lead the audience participation? I'm
            thinking 'Pin the Tail on the Ox' at the
            moment, followed by a chorus of 'Old
            McDonald'. We've got free chocolate turkeys
            from Asda. Costume fittings, please.

ERIC: *(standing at a costume rail and is trying on
            clothes)* My concentration IS all over the
            place!! Is it any wonder? I've got the Civic
            Service to do tomorrow as well, let alone
            the Mother's Union, Midnight Mass, Christmas
            Day sermon and a run round the residential
            home. And she wants me to be looking deep
            within the character of Melchior. I see him
            in red with a golden crown, noble features
            and master of the camel. Yes, he's a bit
            like me really. I look as though I should be
            a leader dressed up in an appropriate
            costume. Underneath, I'm a vicar in my second
            parish with as many insecurities and worries
            as I did on day one of my curacy. No one
            will ever know. *(moves over to centre stage)*

I feel a bit like an actor at times - B-rate
movie of course. I know my lines, most of my
moves and I just love people looking at me,
giving me the plaudits, having my captive
audience listening to me once a week. My
solo performance on my own cosy little
stage, twelve and a half minutes - no more
and no less. Christmas, now that's a big
picture. A show-stopper - people come from
miles around. Not to listen to me - no, I
can kid myself that they are. But I know
it's that crunching through the snow, smell
of candles type of feeling that they are all
coming for. Not for me. But I can dream. I
wanted to be a star - I did really. Not a
'shining star in the East for the nativity'-
type star. No, I really wanted to be a star,
a celebrity, to be famous. Ridiculous.
*(moves back to the dresser and reads a
programme)* And the culmination of my West
End dreams - 'The St Mary's Literary
Society's production of *We Three Sing*, at St
Mary's Church Hall'. Opening and closing in
a matter of twenty-four hours. The reviews

promise to be stunning. You see, I reckon
Melchior liked to be noticed. That's why I
see him turned out in bright red – leading
the camel from across the merciless heat of
the desert. The other two bring tiny little
trinkets for their gifts. Not my man – two
big slabs of solid gold, gleaming like
heaven against the dark background of a
smelly stable. That's my boy. I think Casper
was probably the worrier, with all the
nagging doubts and questions. Balthazar,
he's the pragmatist, feet on the ground,
nothing fancy. We are all wonderfully
typecast, I'll give that to Marjorie. Doreen
is always telling me to 'keep it real, keep
it real, love'. And I wish I could, I really
wish I could. My life, I suppose – it seems
a bit shallow. I don't want to just go
through the motions for the next thirty
years. I mean, don't get me wrong, my faith
is there, it looks good, it really looks
good. *(pause – he takes hold of his gold
bar)* But underneath... well, it's a bit like
this gold bar you see. Looks good *(he
opens)*, but underneath, it's just an old
shoe box. Oh, it's a journey, it's a journey
all right. In miles – nothing like Melchior
and his pals. In complexity – I need a good
map, or a good navigator. I need to get from
being good at my job, to being good at my
faith.

You see, I've got a theory that anyone can
shine like a star. They are so distant some
of them, they seem so unreal. It's only when
you get close up you can see what they
really are. A gaseous mass generating heat
and light. You see, I think people can look
at me and see me centre stage, 'finding the
light' and shining for England. When you get

close up – I don't think I'm generating very
much. No heat, no light. Not enough, anyway.
(blackout)

*Lights fade up. 'In the Bleak Midwinter'; snow
falling. Melchior slowly arrives in costume and lays
his gift, followed by Balthazar and finally Casper who
has forgotten his myrrh. All slowly assume final
position.*

MARJORIE: *(from stalls)* Oh, lovely, lovely! *(they
break from the tableau)* Let's just hold that
final tableau just a moment longer. Lovely –
thanks everyone. I want everyone to take a
quick fifteen-minute break, have some
refreshments and then we'll be ready for our
opening night. Five months in the making –
let's give it everything, everyone! Three
kings, one final voice warm-up if you would,
please.

Wise men quickly sing 'As With Gladness' verse one.

MARJORIE: *(from the audience and coming up onto stage)*
OK, let's all take fifteen minutes please.
Don't be late back! Mrs Myatt has donated
some mince pies, just one each please.
Believe me, one will be enough. All right,
Bernard, house lights please.

House lights up. Interval.

ACT 2

Eric is discovered singing one verse of 'Silent Night' – dressed in evening wear using fifties' style microphone. Mirrorball-type lighting effect on stage.

Music plays under his next speech.

ERIC: *(with mic)* The wise men, after much consultation and stargazing, began their long journey from the east. Where the journey would take them, they didn't exactly know just then. Only that they had to make the long journey. Contrary to some people's view, the kings didn't begin their travelling on the customary camel, oh, no; other modes of transport were readily available. The camel came into its own much later in the story (we hope) – thanks to Abdul's Camel Hire just outside Cairo. Ladies, Gentlemen, boys and girls, welcome to our journey amongst the stars and to *We Three Sing*.

Eric finishes with another verse of 'Silent Night' and exits at the end of the song. Doreen and Brian come on stage riding horses' heads on sticks.

BRIAN: *(pointing and looking left)* Balthazar, we must gather our gifts and move towards the star in the west that guides our paths.

DOREEN: *(looking right)* A wonderful and brilliant sign in the night skies.

Brian notices his mistake and looks where Doreen is looking.

BRIAN: Never have I seen anything to compare with
           it.

DOREEN: He really must be a special baby.

BRIAN: We have not further time to lose, my friend.
           We must quickly climb on to our... er...
           our donkeys and follow the star. Is Melchior
           prepared?

DOREEN: Still wrapping his present!

Music - 'Twinkle, twinkle...' *is heard on the*
keyboard.

SM: *(V/O on tannoy)* Ladies and gentlemen, it's
           time for Round One of 'Pin the Tail on the
           Ox' with your host, Marco Bellini.

Eric appears in TV host jacket. Flashing lights. He
has a hand-held mic.

ERIC: Good evening, everyone, and welcome to a
           very special part of our journey together.
           Yes, it may be very early on in our journey
           together. But it is time for Round One of...
           yes, you guessed it: 'Pin the Tail on the
           Ox'. There you see the back end of our very
           own friendly ox, as yet untouched by human
           hands. Now all I need is a willing volunteer
           to come up and join me here on stage. You
           pop the blindfold on, quick spin round and
           then head for the ox with the tail. Nearest
           to the Bull's... er... Bull's-eye by the end
           of the evening wins a day out at Bristol
           Zoo. Second prize a wonderful blooming
           poinsettia and the booby prize - a plate of
           Mrs Myatt's mince pies. Now, who wants to...

Sound and lights on platform and Eric - crossfade to dressing room and to Doreen and Brian.

DOREEN: You might need a touch more red on your cheeks, Brian, love. She wanted that Mediterranean look, if you remember. Eric resembles someone who has spent the last six weeks in Tenerife.

BRIAN: There's a good number in... for a first night.

DOREEN: Well, they've only got tonight and tomorrow to catch it. Unless that man in the creamy raincoat on the front row is a West End producer waiting to snap us up for a prolonged run.

BRIAN: The man on the left-hand side as you look out?

DOREEN: Yes, I don't recognise him. Do you know him?

BRIAN: Tom Innes, a colleague of mine from work.

DOREEN: Oh, I see. Good that he could come. I'm pretty sure everyone else are St Mary's folk.

BRIAN: He's just finished going through a messy divorce. Not sure if he was going to see much of his kids at Christmas. He was good to me when Mum died, so I've just been investing a bit of time with him, I suppose. Told him about what we had going on over Christmas and here he is.

DOREEN: That's great, Brian. Good for you.

BRIAN: Bit embarrassing really. He's used to seeing me in a pinstriped suit, burying my head in

some corporate figures. Not in a green sheet
and carrying a horse's head on a stick.

DOREEN: You'll be the talk of the staffroom come
Monday.

BRIAN: I doubt it. Besides, I'm off now until the
fourth of Jan. Is there any news of the
camel, by the way?

DOREEN: Thankfully not, although Marjorie is still
hoping it will arrive prior to our entrance
into Bethlehem. Last I heard, it had stopped
at some services on the M5 for refreshments.

SM: (V/O on tannoy) Stand-by for the Cairo
nightclub scene please... 'Betty Bouston and
the Dance of the 107 Veils' to the stage
please.

DOREEN: Do they all know about this at the office,
then, Brian?

BRIAN: Yes... yes, I prefer to tell them. I didn't
want them coming across a photograph in the
Chronicle with me sat on a camel or kneeling
in the manger or whatever.

DOREEN: What about coming to St Mary's? Do they know
about you being treasurer and things?

BRIAN: Yes... yes, they do. I tell everyone who I
think might be interested. And one or two
who aren't. Don't you?

DOREEN: (pause) Not always, no, I don't.

BRIAN: Listen, I better go. I promised I'd watch
Betty from the wings.

DOREEN: Oh yes.

BRIAN: She's a bit worried about the belly dancing
            routine in front of the mayor.

DOREEN: I shouldn't worry; he'll be sound asleep by
            now, if he's got any sense. He looked a bit
            drowsy during the overture.

Eric comes in - crossing Brian exiting.

ERIC: Betty's on. Bernard pressed the wrong
            button. For a moment she was doing the
            'Dance of the 107 Veils' to the sound of
            'Frosty the Snowman'.

DOREEN: He's not far off - it's freezing back stage.

ERIC: The boiler's not working. At this rate we
            could easily have saved money on imitation
            snow.

DOREEN: How did round one of 'Pin the Tail' go?

ERIC: Not a huge success, little Tony Bradshaw got
            slightly disorientated and stumbled onto the
            wings, plunging the tail into Eileen
            Birdfoot's thigh. If the audience didn't
            know we had a prompter before they certainly
            do now. Never heard such a scream.

DOREEN: Mr Barker awake again?

ERIC: Still snoring beautifully, in a slightly
            different key to His Worship the Mayor.
            Brian seemed in a rush; he's not got a cameo
            in the dance routine, has he?

DOREEN: He'd promised Betty Bouston he'd watch the
            'Dance of the 107 Veils'. Now, Betty and
            Brian would make a lovely couple. They could
            do dance routines together. Next year's
            panto - or maybe in church.

ERIC: Brian doesn't dance. And Mrs Viney certainly
            doesn't approve of dance in church.

DOREEN: What does she approve of? I can't believe
            she's here tonight and on the front row.

ERIC: As you well know, she runs the bookshop and
            church lending library. I think she saw the
            chance of a few sales in the Interval.

DOREEN: I can sense her glare, every time I come on.
            Surely she can't object to an eastern king
            wearing a pair of open-toed sandals.

ERIC: She can object to most things. She took
            great pleasure yesterday in telling me that
            for the second year running the book that
            has been borrowed the most from the library
            has been *101 Things to Do During a Dull
            Sermon*. She smiled sweetly and she said it
            as though I might be interested in the news.

DOREEN: Not a bad book actually.

Brian dashes back.

BRIAN: We're on... 'Ding Dong Dance Routine' in the
            Cairo Kasbah.

*They rush to the platform and do a perfect rendition
of the 'Ding Dong Dance Routine'. Brian's 'Riverdance'
is still in. They all exit to rapturous applause.
Music Fill for thirty seconds with lights changing to
night lighting.*

BRIAN: *(looking and pointing right)* Another six
            hours and we should be on the outskirts of
            Bethlehem.

ERIC: *(looking left)* The star is certainly getting
            brighter. *(Brian notices and corrects his
            mistake)* Maybe Bethlehem is the place where
            the King is to be born.

DOREEN: Then let's get some rest. We have a long day
            tomorrow. Are the camels secured, Casper?

BRIAN: *(pointing off stage)* Why, yes. I can see
            them now at the oasis. *(shouting)* C'mon now,
            lie down there, get some sleep.

ERIC: *(muttering)* What a wonderful way with
            animals you have, Casper.

Lights are fading.

DOREEN: Goodnight Melchior, goodnight Casper!

ERIC: Goodnight Balthazar, goodnight Casper.

BRIAN: Goodnight, Balthazar. Goodnight... *(dries)*

ERIC: *(whispers)* Melchior.

BRIAN: Aye, Melchior.

ERIC: *(quietly)* Goodnight Jim-Bob.

*Lights cross to stage right – Fingers Freddie on
keyboard plays and Marjorie sings 'Little Donkey' –
whilst the horses' heads make an appearance through
the curtains upstaging the song. Song finishes and
lights cross to dressing room.*

BRIAN: I've been giving the trip to Scotland a bit
            of a thought. I know it's a bit late notice
            but I'm thinking I might stay around here
            now. Not definite yet, I'd only booked a
            cheap B&B but the train fare was a bit

costly. Betty's doing a lunchtime cabaret on
Christmas Day at Ashleigh Old People's Home.
She asked me to link the event through,
maybe do a quick monologue. Now, I did ask
myself very carefully, 'Am I just saying yes
because someone has asked me very sweetly?'
But actually no, I realise that it's maybe
something I really want to do. It's not that
I've caught the showbiz bug; in fact, I know
I haven't. Well, it's just that Betty's not
doing any family thing until Boxing Day, so
she'll be on her own and I won't be crashing
into anyone's family Christmas... And, well,
I'll get a good dinner out of the Home.
Betty said I could go back to hers in the
evening for some mulled wine, watch a bit of
television. Apparently, Mrs Myatt has given
her a plate of mince pies. I spoke to Doreen
about it. She seems very keen that I stay

around. She said I could come around to
their place on Boxing Day and entertain
their cousin Keith from Blackburn. I will
miss not seeing the lights but it's like
Doreen says, maybe 'it's the kind of
experience that's better shared, and I ought
to think of taking someone up there with me
next year'. She's full of good ideas,
Doreen; always buys unusual presents at
Christmas. She's already told me what I'm
getting this year – six dance lessons at the
local college, a pair of twinkly tap shoes
and Michael Flatley's autobiography. Think
she might be trying to tell me something.

Lights fade on dressing room.

SM: *(V/O on tannoy)* Ladies and gentlemen! It's
time for Round Two of 'Pin the Tail on the
Ox' – with your host, Marco Bellini!

Eric enters – music and flashing lights.

ERIC: Hi, and welcome back to round two of your
favourite 'Pin the Tail on the Ox'. And to
help us, here is my lovely and glamorous
assistant Vanessa. *(Brian enters with donkey
and promptly exits as Vanessa enters)* Yes,
looking a picture of elegance in a long gown
and open-toed scandals, it is the ever
popular – Vanessa. Let's give her a round of
applause. Now, we have big prizes today.
So who's going to be next to 'Pin the Tail
on the Ox'?

*The game is played – Vanessa gets two volunteers from
the audience. After game, exit to music sting.*

Crossfade to stage left dressing room. Brian is rehearsing a monologue for Christmas Day.

BRIAN: 'Twas the night before Christmas, when all
            through the house,
            Not a creature was stirring, not even a
            (pause) mouse
            The stockings were hung by the chimney with
            care
            In hopes that St Nicholas would soon be
            there.

Eric and Doreen enter.

ERIC: Sounded good, Brian. Is Casper going it
            alone now?

BRIAN: No, no, it's just something I'm hoping to
            put together for Christmas – for the lunch
            at Ashleigh House.

DOREEN: That's nice, Brian. You've decided to do it,
            then?

BRIAN: Yes, I think so. Besides, the weather
            forecast for Scotland is not very promising.
            So it looks as though I might be seeing you
            on Boxing Day. If that's still all right
            with you both.

ERIC: Fine with us, just avoid cousin Keith when
            it comes to party games, and try not to get
            into any long conversations with Uncle Bill.
            You can't miss him – he'll be the one
            wearing a hideous tie.

DOREEN: It's a bit of a madhouse, but you'll be very
            welcome. You can ask Betty to join us if
            she's not doing anything.

ERIC: Doreen!

DOREEN: Well why not? Nothing wrong with inviting a
          friend, now, is there?

BRIAN: She always visits family on Boxing Day. But
          thank you, I'll mention it to her that she
          was invited.

ERIC: Tell her that her Auntie Doreen approves of
          her and hopes you will both be very happy.

DOREEN: Now you're being ridiculous, Eric.

BRIAN: It's all right. There's nothing to gossip
          about, I can assure you. We both just value
          a bit of companionship at the moment.

DOREEN: And I think that's lovely, Brian, I really
          do. And just think, you've both got such a
          lot in common as well.

BRIAN: Have we?

ERIC   Have they?

DOREEN: Well, you will have, come Christmas Day.
          You'll both have a matching pair of twinkly
          tap shoes. I bought Betty a pair for
          Christmas last year, size seven, sky blue
          with white dots.

BRIAN: How did the 'Pin the Tail on the Ox' part
          two end up?

ERIC: I think we're getting there. I'm not sure
          what Health and Safety would have to say
          about it. One of the kids nearly stumbled
          into the orchestra pit by mistake.
          His so-called mates were guiding him with
          their helpful instructions.

DOREEN: Any news on Omar, love?

ERIC: Apparently, he had something that disagreed
          with him at the services. They've had to
          make an urgent stop on the hard shoulder.
          And if he does arrive, they suggest he has
          his own dressing room and no one's to stand
          down wind of him for some time.

DOREEN: Charming – are we nearly on?

ERIC: The shepherds are just coming down off the
          hills and then it's us with Herod.

BRIAN: I think I might go and watch the shepherds.
          I love watching their faces when the angel
          appears. Must have been a very special
          moment.

*Crossfade to Fingers Freddie on keyboard. Marjorie
sings three verses of 'While Shepherds Watch Their
Flocks by Night'. Crossfade back to Doreen on her own
in dressing room.*

DOREEN: Deborah rang last night. It seems they want
          to come to the matinee tomorrow and then
          talk about Christmas arrangements. I felt
          sure she was going to say they couldn't make
          it on Boxing Day. But no, not only are they
          coming but they want to stay overnight and
          spend the following day with us. It seems
          Dominic, their eldest, finds Eric hilarious
          and says it's a happy relief following
          Christmas Day at Clive's parents. Clive's
          mother reads Christmas poetry for forty
          minutes following dinner, and then they sit
          down, make themselves comfortable and listen
          to extracts of Handel's *Messiah* for an hour
          and a half before a buffet tea.

Father rang up and said that he and Mother were very much looking forward to being with us on Boxing Day. They heard that Debs and Clive were staying over and so have decided to do likewise. 'But please – please don't worry about accommodation.' They've booked themselves into the Fairlawns Hotel. Special price if you stay three days. Mother then came on the phone and said it wasn't only me who has unusual ideas for Christmas presents. They had found just the thing for Eric and I – a new shower unit, a fluffy rug for the lounge, a bath mat and a set of new curtains for the front room. 'Thank you, Mother,' I said, 'always thinking of us.'

Back to stage right. Fifties style song – Marjorie singing 'Rudolf the Red Nosed Reindeer'. Audience joins in. Pause. Marjorie removes red nose and addresses audience.

MARJORIE: I know they are all probably making fun of me now. Doesn't worry me really. I've had fun made out of me for years, particularly on stage. Who can forget my first role in the Sunday school nativity? Most people who saw it tried to forget it very quickly. I know Mrs Doomsday, the leader of the children's group 'Mini-Snappers', still has sleepless nights over it. At the time I thought a live sheep would be just the thing for the manger scene. Unfortunately Lulu, the docile ewe, lasted only two minutes on the stage and then far too enthusiastically took an interest in the lady mayoress's new hat. Once Lulu had finished nibbling on the hat, she got far too excited in the centre aisle, leaving various deposits and an aroma that gave a rustic and realistic atmosphere

to the whole evening. The mayor apparently
trod in something rather unpleasant that he
was to keep with him over Christmas and well
into the New Year. The bill for his shoes
and a new hat for his wife was twice as much
as the box office takings. Mrs Doomsday
moved away from the area quickly with, as
she put it, her 'reputation and any hopes of
the West End in tatters'.

I did send her a gentle invitation to the
premiere of *We Three Sing*. When she heard
there was a possibility of a live camel
being part of the proceedings, she
apparently quickly booked a two-week
Christmas break in Torremolinos and sent me
a polite apology. *(Marjorie moves centre
stage)*

It's a place to live out your dreams,
though, isn't it? The stage, I mean. One
minute I'm an assistant behind the counter
in the Bakers Oven, filling a meringue and
boxing up custard tarts. The next I'm under
make-up and lights and playing characters
and saying lines I would never be able to do
or say in real life. The thing is, I prefer
it to real life – always have done really.
Escaping reality, I suppose. By the time
Monday comes it will be back to serving
bloomers and sausage rolls by day and
preparing for the Palm Sunday extravaganza
by night. I'm already making tentative
enquiries about a live mule for the opening
scene.

I think that's why I probably enjoy
Christmas so much; well, you know how it is,
nothing seems real for a few days. All
tinsel and trifle and titbits. I end up

going to no end of parties and 'drinks' with
all sorts of people I don't really know.
I won't see most of them for another twelve
months. Just another chance to perform,
I suppose. Bit like the after-show party
tomorrow. Linda at work was very kind, she
let me have two dozen mushroom vol-au-vents
for nothing – they only passed their sell-by
date last Wednesday. Should still look OK –
the lighting's very bad in the small back
hall. No one will complain after three
glasses of Mr Trouper's home-made punch.
They're more likely to be totally incoherent
or in a heap on the table tennis table.
(Marjorie moves back stage right)

All right – quickly Brian, it's time for
Casper by night scene – bring your horse
love. OK Bernard, night lighting please...

Total blackout.

Not quite what I had in mind...

*Cross to Brian, as Casper, on platform, carrying his
horse head on a stick, now in proper night lighting.*

BRIAN: A brilliant star. *(Brian looks left and
right before deciding on right)* You couldn't
miss it. Nearly there now. It's getting
brighter all the time. The others are just
tying up the camels for the night. We'll be
in Bethlehem this time tomorrow. I just
wanted to come out and take a final look at
the night sky. *(spins the horse's head to
look up and then back down)* It's amazing to
think that these stars will still be being
looked at years after we've gone –
a thousand, two thousand years from now.

Amazing. I just get a very special feeling being out here. Tomorrow will be something unique... I'm convinced of that. Whether they'll be talking about me and the other two in a couple of thousand years or not, I don't know. Don't really care if they're not. But what happens tomorrow, that's history in the making that is, no doubt about that.

Right down the ages there'll be people like me coming out just like this on a cold winter's night – and thanking God for what's going to happen tomorrow night. That same God who made all the stars. And that's special, very special. Thank you. *(lights fade)*

Lights up on dressing room – Eric and Doreen are in there, Eric on mobile phone.

ERIC: Oh right. Right, I see... well, thanks anyway. Bye. *(to Doreen)* The news on Omar is not good. Major traffic jam around junction thirteen.

DOREEN: What a shame. I'm sure no one's noticed. Brian with his horse on a stick has a certain charm about it.

ERIC: You never know, he might get here for the curtain calls. There's always tomorrow and the matinee.

DOREEN: No – afraid not. He was cut from the matinee during a Health and Safety meeting yesterday. They were afraid the kiddies screaming would startle the delicate little thing.

ERIC: So he's coming all this way and not likely to be seen by anyone.

DOREEN: Not exactly – Marjorie's got him making an
            impromptu appearance in Woolworth's grotto
            tomorrow morning as a publicity stunt.
            Half-past ten if you're interested.

ERIC: Never misses a trick, does she? By the way,
            I've picked up a message on the mobile.
            Denise and John are definitely coming Boxing
            Day – and any chance of staying on a couple
            of days?

DOREEN: They've been speaking to Mother.

ERIC: She just said that she and John would
            understand if it was a squeeze – but they
            just love the special Christmassy feel there
            is here – and wanted to stay a bit longer
            this year.

DOREEN: Oh... I see.

ERIC: I haven't replied. It's you. You know that,
            don't you? You're a wonderful hostess, making
            time for everyone. And you keep that family
            together, all of them. You do, really.

DOREEN: Not sure about that.

ERIC: Well, they are... that's why they're all
            heading this way over Christmas.

DOREEN: Do you mind?

ERIC: Course not. I'm very proud of you. (they
            embrace) Besides, I get you the rest of the
            year, now, don't I?

DOREEN: Are you all ready?

ERIC: Ready?

DOREEN: Pre-Boxing Day madness?

ERIC: Mother's Union talk – no need now, Brian is
               coming with me and will wow them with his
               stargazing extravaganza. Non-threatening
               little talk for Christmas Eve all done and
               ready. Christmas Day sermon – still not sure
               but might focus in on the 'Wonder of the
               Season'. Get a few kids to bring their gifts
               to the front. Probably makes sense to talk
               about the wise men – the 'Star of Wonder'-
               type angle.

DOREEN: Sounds great, love.

ERIC: Then a quick dash round Ashleigh House in a
               Santa outfit, a few quick ho, ho, ho's and
               back home just in time for Christmas dinner
               with you, me and Her Majesty in the
               background.

SM: *(V/O on tannoy)* 'Three Kings Shadows
               Routine' to the stage please.

DOREEN: Quick, that's us.

*Fingers Freddie on keyboard. Three wise men on
platform sing 'We Three Kings'. Each wise man sings a
verse at the microphone – Melchior, Balthazar then
Caspar. Each verse is acted out by the other wise
men. Song finishes.*

Lights up stage left – dressing room. Eric comes in.

ERIC: I always used to enjoy those Miss Marple
               specials over Christmas, or *Poirot*. Don't seem
               to get these any more! A good 'whodunit'.
               It's all game shows and soaps on Christmas
               Day now. I'm going to have to watch it; I'm
               beginning to sounds like Doreen's mother.

I've booked a long weekend away in January
just for Doreen and myself. A little holiday
cottage in Cornwall – miles from anywhere. It
seems busier then ever this year. Probably
this show hasn't helped. It's manic. I must
be doing something right, or one of us is.
It seems everyone is wanting to pop in at
some time or other over the next few days.
I've decided to change my talk for Christmas
Day. I'm going to talk about the gift of
hospitality, about welcoming strangers, about
looking out for others. I'm going to get the
others involved – Balthazar and Casper; well,
Doreen and Brian anyway. Doreen just has an
open door at home – anyone's welcome at any
time. I don't mind; I said when we arrived
here, I want people to be able to talk to me
about anything and they didn't need an
appointment to do so. Well, me – or Doreen.
That's how I see it. We're a team. Pretty
good one too, I think.

And Brian's a star. *(laughs)* Well, he
probably wants to be. Doreen's already
thinking about his present for next year. She
wants to get a star named after him. I didn't
know you could, but she's already making
enquiries. What you see is what you get with
Brian and people like that. He's got a number
of people to come and see the show, and
there's often someone there on a Sunday
because of Brian. He's a good man. He's never
in a rush, always finds time for you. His
faith is real, very personal. Maybe that's
what I need in the New Year – just to slow
up, take my time, invest in the things that
really matter. I need to do that – I really
do. *(Mobile phone rings in his bag – he finds
it)* Hello, Eric Wiseman speaking, yes, yes...
oh, OK. Yes, you turn left at the first set

of lights, over a little bridge, then second
on the left. You should see the church just
after that and the hall is just beyond it on
the right. All right, yes, hope to see you
shortly... yes, bye-now. *(shouts off stage)*
It's Omar, he's on his way – you should be
able to spot him or smell him in about ten
minutes. *(runs off stage)*

*Marjorie sings first verse of 'Hark the Herald' with
Freddie.*

*'In the Bleak Midwinter' playing in background. Wise
men assume positions on platform. Snow is falling.*

ERIC: We bring gifts of gold, frankincense and
            myrrh to our new King.

DOREEN: We have travelled by... er... by... *(looking
            into the wing, hopefully)* the light of the
            guiding star which has brought us here.

BRIAN: We worship you, King of kings. We travel
            back by a different route, so we don't have
            to recount our story to Harold – er...
            Herod.

ERIC: Our God, heaven cannot hold Him,
            nor earth sustain
            Heaven and earth shall flee away
            When He comes to reign.
            In the bleak midwinter
            a stable-place sufficed
            The Lord God Almighty,
            Jesus Christ.

DOREEN: Angels and archangels
May have gathered there,
Cherubim and seraphim
Thronged the air.
But His mother only,
In her maiden bliss,
Worshipped the Beloved
With a kiss.

BRIAN: What can I give Him,
Poor as I am?
If I were a shepherd,
I would bring a lamb.
If I were a wise man,
I would do my part;
Yet what I can I give Him –
Give my heart.

DOREEN: I can give my heart.

ERIC: I can give my heart.

Wise men come together and sing one verse of 'As with Gladness Men of Old' – similar to opening scene. Doreen gets her harmony right. Bows are taken. Doreen and Brian exit.

ERIC: Thank you so much for coming. We all do appreciate you being here this evening. Many thanks of course to my fellow travellers, Doreen and Brian together with Fingers Freddie on the keyboard and all our technical crew. And, in particular, the wonderfully patient and inspiring Marjorie Lockwood, our director. Let's give her a round of applause.

Marjorie comes on and takes a bow – and is given a bouquet of flowers.

ERIC: We are here tomorrow, of course, for the
           matinee - then church services on Christmas
           Eve and Christmas Day. Please try to come
           and see us over the festive season - you'll
           get a very warm welcome. And maybe a chance
           to discover again why the wise men travelled
           so far, why they were so full of wonder and
           awe and why these tales have lived on
           through so many generations. *(he goes to the
           mic)* Thank you again for coming - Doreen,
           Brian and I will be in the foyer afterwards.
           Please feel free to stay and have a chat,
           and I do understand there are plenty of Mrs
           Myatt's mince pies left over, so please help
           yourselves. Good night and have a very happy
           Christmas.

*Eric sings 'Silent Night' again one verse - swirling
lights effect. As they finish, Omar comes charging
through the curtains onto platform - caught in lights
for a moment - then blackout. Finish. Music.*

THREE WISE MEN AND A BABY

TECHNICAL SYNOPSIS

Please note these technical suggestions are only to be taken as guidelines, and will be determined by your own budget and venue limitations. If you want further details or are interested in hiring any of the gear, you can contact Saltmine via the website – www.saltmine.org/sts.

The set

The set consist of three spaces:

The stage left (SL) space is set out as a dressing room with a table with dressing room mirror (square of wood with square painted silver in centre) with lights around it. This can be wired up to work as practical. There are two chairs, one at the end of the table, the other facing the mirror. There is a costume rail set at the back of the area with random bits of costume that the cast change into and large hamper in front of the rail with various props and costumes piled in it.

The centre stage (CS) area is a raised platform riser 8ft by 8ft by 1ft high. The sides are blacked out; at the back, a red curtain is hung from a pole which is clipped onto two uprights screwed to the back of the platform. This is the 'stage' that the characters in the play use.

Stage right (SR) during Act 1 is set as 'the vicarage' with two comfy living room chairs, a coffee table, a bookcase at the back and a Christmas tree (the Christmas tree lights can be wired up to work as practical). During Act 2 it becomes the orchestra pit, with a keyboard with a mic, a boom mic stand, and a straight mic stand with a large 1950s mic for the characters to sing from; a larger Christmas tree is set at the back.

A chair is placed just to the side of the set, or in the front row of the audience, for the character director to sit in.

The black drape across the back of the set is a star-cloth which is used in Act 2.

All stage directions are from the perspective of the actor looking out to the auditorium from the stage.

Back stage

Up Stage Right (USR)	Up Stage Centre (USC)	Up Stage Left (USL)
Stage Right (SR)	Stage Centre (SC)	Stage Left (SL)
Down Stage Right (DSR)	Down Stage Centre (DSC)	Down Stage Left (DSL)

Auditorium

SFX and LX (Sound Effects and Lighting Effects)

Sound plot

ACT 1

SFX 1: pre-show music

SFX 2: fade out pre-show

(when cued)

SFX 3: pre-show announcement

(when pre-show music has faded)

SFX 4:   'Little Donkey' track

(Marjorie '. . . it'll soon be Christmas')

SFX 5: fade out 'Little Donkey'

(when Doreen set SR)

SFX 6:   'We Three Kings' track

(Eric '. . . wise men were really searching for')

SFX 7: fade 'We Three Kings' track

(when Brian set CS)

SFX 8: 'Rocking Around the Christmas Tree' track

(Brian '. . . Still searching')

SFX 9: fade 'Rocking Around the Christmas Tree' track

(when Doreen set SR)

SFX 10: snap 'Ding Dong Dance Routine' track plays out

(Marjorie '. . . places on stage')

SFX 11: thunder SFX 'LOUD!!'

(Marjorie '. . . Places, everyone')

SFX 12: 'O Little Town of Bethlehem' track

(Doreen '. . . Still searching')

SFX 13: 'Silent Night' track

(as Doreen and Brian hug)

SFX 14: 'In the Bleak Midwinter' choir track

(Eric '. . . Not enough, anyway')

SFX 15: Interval music

(when house lights are up)

Interval

ACT 2

SFX 16: fade Interval music

(when cast ready for Act 2)

SFX 17: keyboard live, and SR fifties mic live, mute at end of song

(when house lights have faded)

SFX 18: 'Twinkle, Twinkle' track plays to cover end of scene, game show sting with V/O (voice off), radio mic live and game show background music live (Doreen 'Wrapping his present')

SFX 19: fade game show music

(Eric '. . . Now who wants to. . .')

SFX 20: 'Arabian Belly Dance' track plays out

(stage manager ". . . 107 Veils" to the stage please')

SFX 21: 'Ding Dong Dance Routine' track plays out

(Brian '". . . Routine" in the Cairo Kasbah')

SFX 22: V/O game show intro with game show music

(with blackout)

SFX 23: fade game show music

(when Eric exits)

SFX 24: keyboard live and fifties mic mute at end of song

(Doreen '. . . always thinking of us')

SFX 25: keyboard live

(Doreen 'Quick, that's us')

SFX 26: 'mobile phone ring' track

(Eric '. . . I need to do that – I really do')

SFX 27: keyboard and mic live mute at end of song

(Eric '. . . in about ten minutes')

SFX 28: 'In the Bleak Midwinter' choir track

(at the end of the song after lights fade)

SFX 29: keyboard and mic live mute at end of song

(Eric '. . . have a very happy Christmas' or as he moves across)

SFX 30: pre-show music

(with house lights)

Tracks, music and sound equipment needed

Effects tracks include:

'Little Donkey' track

'We Three Kings' track

'Rocking Around the Christmas Tree' track

'Ding Dong Dance Routine' track

Thunder SFX

Quieter 'Little Donkey' track or similar simple Christmas track

'Silent Night' track

'In the Bleak Midwinter' choir track

Game show music

'Arabian Belly Dance' track

'Mobile Phone ring' track

V/O can either be live or recorded (SM/character)

Most of the tracks used during the original production are from the following CDs:

It's a Trad Jazz Christmas
Jazzenda
EMI Gold
ASIN B0000AOWV4

We also use these CDs for walk-in music.

A keyboard and stand, a vocal mic on a boom stand, a straight mic stand, a fifties-looking mic (we use a SHURE 55SH-2); and a hand-held radio mic for the game show.

Lighting plot

ACT 1

LX 1:   pre-show state, house lights

LX 2:   pre-show state, fade house lights

LX 3:   fade pre-show state

LX 4:   fade up CS general wash (plus Marjorie special if needed)

      (The cast sings 'As with Gladness Men of Old')

LX 5:   fade to B/O

      (Marjorie '. . . and remember, it'll soon be Christmas')

LX 6:   lights fade up on SR 'vicarage' general warm wash

      (wait till Doreen is set in chair then fade up)

LX 7:   fade to B/O

      (Eric '. . . what the wise men were really searching for')

LX 8:   fade up CS special and Marjorie special

      (when Brian and Marjorie are set)

LX 9:   snap to CS general wash

      (Marjorie 'Lovely, Brian. . .')

LX 10:   fade to B/O

      (Marjorie '. . . yourself and your character')

LX 11:   fade up SL general warm wash plus mirror lights

      (when Brian set)

LX 12:   fade to B/O

      (Brian '. . . Still searching, Lord . . . Still searching')

LX 13: fade up SR

(when Eric and Doreen are set)

LX 14: snap B/O

(Eric '. . . of course')

LX 15: chase sequence CS low general wash, just so we can see them at all times, including Marjorie

(as music starts)

LX 16: snap B/O

(end of dance routine)

LX 17: fade up SL

(when Brian is set)

LX 18: snap B/O

(Marjorie '. . . Places everyone')

LX 19: fade up sinister light CS reds, green etc

(after thunder sfx)

LX 20: snap to CS general wash

(as Marjorie joins Eric on stage 'Lovely, darling. . .'

LX 21: B/O

(Eric reacts to Marjorie's statement about 'tap dance' and heads off stage)

LX 22: fade up SL

(Doreen is set)

LX 23: B/O

(Doreen '. . . I'm still searching')

LX 24: fade up CS general

(when cast is set CS)

LX 25: B/O

(Brian and Doreen hug)

LX 26: fade up CS general

(Marjorie set CS)

LX 27: crossfade to SL

(Marjorie '. . . Costume fittings please')

LX 28: fade up CS drop SL low

(Eric '. . . No one will ever know' or as he looks like he's going to move across)

LX 29: fade out CS fade SL back to full

(visual on Eric moving back across)

LX 30: B/O

(Eric '. . . no light. Not enough, anyway')

LX 31: slow fade up star-cloth and CS night blue back light and low CS special and snow machine

(as 'In the Bleak Midwinter' plays)

LX 32: snap to CS general

(Marjorie 'Oh, lovely, lovely')

LX 33: snap back to CS night

(Marjorie '. . . just a moment longer')

LX 34: fade back to CS general

(Marjorie '. . . Lovely, thanks everyone')

LX 35: fade down CS general to pre show fade up house lights

(Marjorie '. . . All right, Bernard, house lights please.')

Interval

ACT 2

LX 36: fade house lights and pre show

(when cast ready for Act 2)

LX 37: spot mirrorball, SR special on fifties mic, star-cloth, you may wish to add smoke

(when Eric is ready and music starts)

LX 38: crossfade to CS night with star-cloth

(Eric '. . . and to "We Three Sing"')

LX 39: B/O

(Doreen 'Still wrapping his present')

LX 40: flashing star-cloth, chasing lights, moving lights chase

(V/O 'Ladies and gentlemen . . .')

LX 41: stop all chases, keep star-cloth on, CS general

(Eric enters as Marco Bellini)

LX 42: B/O

(Eric '. . . Now who wants to . . .')

LX 43: fade up SL

(Doreen and Brian set)

LX 44: CS chase, moving lights chase

(as 'Ding Dong Dance' music starts)

LX 45: B/O

(at the end of the dance)

LX 46: fade up CS night with star-cloth

(when cast set CS)

LX 47: slow fade then snap B/O

(fade as they say goodnight to each other snap on 'Jim-Bob')

LX 48: fade up special SR plus low general SR

(when keyboard is set)

LX 49: crossfade to SL

(when song ends and Brian is set)

LX 50: B/O

(Brian '. . . trying to tell me something')

LX 51: Flashing star-cloth, chasing stage lights, moving lights chase

(V/O 'Ladies and gentlemen . . .')

LX 52: Stop all chases, keep star-cloth on, CS general

(Eric enters as Marco Bellini . . .)

LX 53: B/O

(when Marco takes bow and leaves)

LX 54: fade up SL

(when Brian is set)

LX 55:   crossfade to SR keyboard for comedy effect use smoke when inappropriate!

(Brian '. . . very special moment')

LX 56:   crossfade to SL

(when song ends)

LX 57:   B/O

(Doreen '. . . always thinking of us')

LX 58:   fade up SR mic special dim red wash and red mirrorball

(when keyboard is set)

LX 59:   crossfade to SR general

(song ends)

LX 60:   fade up CS general fade SR to dim

(as Marjorie moves across)

LX 61:   fade down CS fade up SR general

(Marjorie moves SR)

LX 62:   snap B/O

(Marjorie '. . . night lighting please')

LX 63:   fade up CS night with star–cloth

(Brian enters CS)

LX 64:   B/O

(Brian '. . . Thank you')

LX 65:   fade up SL

(Doreen is set)

LX 66: crossfade to CS general and low SR add SR mic special as cast use the mic

(Doreen '. . . Quick, that's us')

LX 67: B/O

(song ends)

LX 68: fade up SL

(Eric enters SL)

LX 69: crossfade to SR keyboard

(Eric '. . . in about ten minutes')

LX 70: B/O

(song ends)

LX 71: CS night and CS special low, with stars and snow machine

(as 'Bleak Midwinter' plays)

LX 72: fade up CS general slow

(as they sing)

LX 73: snap to SR special plus mirrorball and stars. Add smoke

(as Eric moves to mic)

LX 74: B/O

(end of song)

LX 75: swirly effect on curtain, flashing stars cloth

(after Eric exits)

LX 76: CS full then B/O after 2-4 seconds

(Omar appears!)

LX 77: pre show state and house lights.

Lighting Design for Original Production

Equipment used

12–14 Fresnels (wash lights)

2–3 Spotlights (third for Marjorie's chair if needed)

Smoke Machine (place behind large Christmas tree towards keyboard)

Snow Machine (rigged above SR or SL pointing over riser)

3 Star–cloths

Mirrorball (rigged over riser)

2 Moving head profiles (on the floor DSR and DSL)

Patch

Label	Colour	Focus
SR	205	SR wash, 2 or 3 lamps
CS Amber	179	CS wash, 2 lamps
CS Red	106	CS wash, 2 lamps
CS Blue	363	CS wash, 2 lamps from on stage
CS Open White	OW	CS wash, 2 lamps
SL	205	SL wash, 2 or 3 lamps
SR Spot	OW	Microphone special, tight, sharp
CS Spot	205	DCS special, wide, sharp
Xmas Tree Lights	N/A	N/A
Dressing room lights	N/A	N/A
Smoke	N/A	N/A
Snow	N/A	N/A
Stars	N/A	N/A

NOTE: All numbers are 'LEE Filters' numbers; OW is open white.

Subs/Chases

Sub	Label	Contents
1	SR General	All SL lamps + Xmas tree lights
2	CS General	Mix of CS OW + Amber to give bright warm
3	SL General	All SR lamps + Dressing room lights @ 50%
4	Sinister	Red CS + Green from moving heads + CS special fill
5	Mirrorball	Mirrorball hit by moving heads in OW
6	Red Mirrorball	Mirrorball in Red + CS Red
7	Night	CS Blue + Blue wash from moving heads + CS Special fill + low stars
C1	Game intro	Spring, roaming, bouncing gobos from moving heads + CS colour chase
9	Game static	Moving heads giving house light with prismed gobos + CS bright + stars
10	3 Kings	SR @ 40% + Xmas tree lights + CS Amber + stars
11	Pre-state	(SL + CS Amber + SR + Xmas tree lights + dressing room lights) @ 20%
C2	Star chase	Twinkling star-cloth chase

If you need to hire any equipment such as props and costumes, star-cloths, moving heads and profiles, smoke machines or snow machines, these can be hired from Saltmine Technical Services on 01384 454823 or www.saltmine.org.

Set design and lighting design are by Saltmine Technical Services.
Technical synopsis by Saltmine Technical Services.

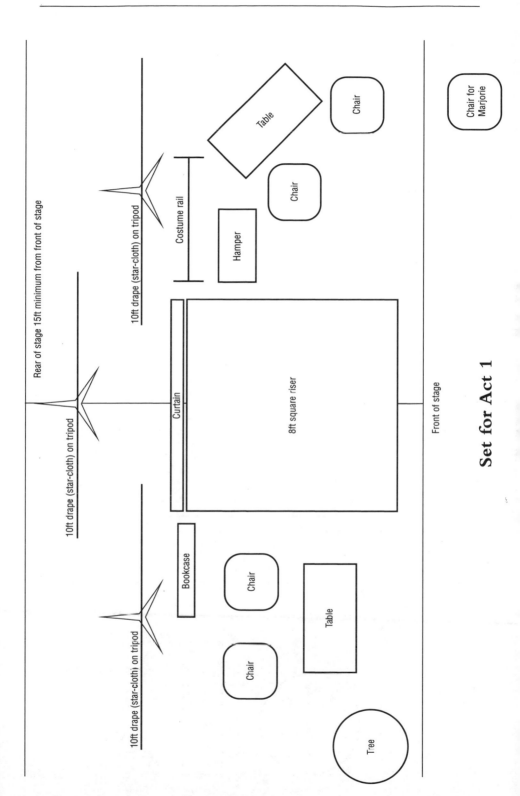

Set for Act 1

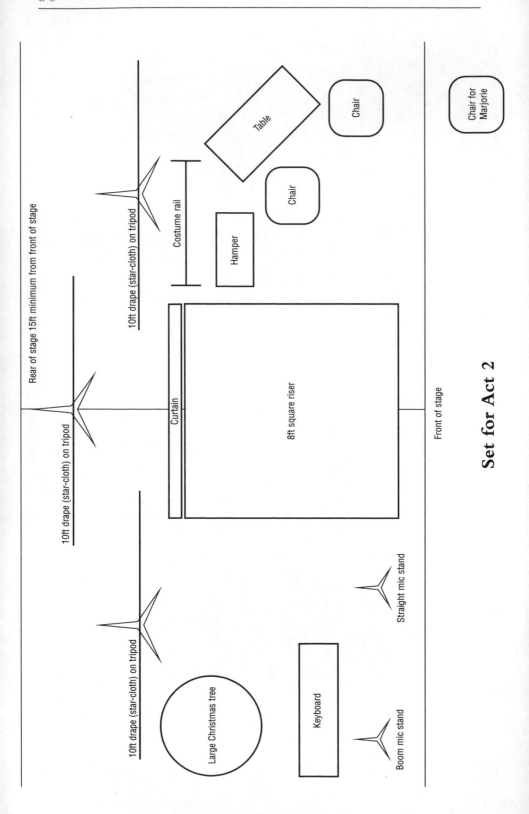

Set for Act 2

A CHRISTMAS SPECIAL
By David Robinson

CAST:
Reverend Vernon Spore

Enter Revd. Vernon Spore. Goes to lectern.

REVD. SPORE:

> I want to talk to you this evening about that age-old 'hazelnut roasting on the gas fire' Christmas.
>
> It first became a burden to me a couple of years ago whilst I was relaxing in front of the television watching the closing moments of the *Bonnie Langford Christmas Special*. And I thought to myself then, as I think to myself now, 'What does all this mean? What is it about?' And 'How much does she get paid?'
>
> And it put me in mind of the sort of question I want to ask you this evening: 'What does Bonnie Langford mean to you?'... Er, no, I'm sorry, er... 'What does Christmas mean to you?' Or should I say, 'What could Christmas mean to you?'
>
> I want, if I may, to split my address into three sections this evening – Crackers, Chestnuts and Cranberry Sauce.
>
> It all began many years ago in a backyard stable in the little town of Bethlehem. They were in the stable because there was no room for them at the inn. Nothing very surprising about that, you might say – hotels are always busy at Christmas.

But then, something rather surprising did begin to happen - visitors from afar. Again you might say to me, we all get visitors at Christmas. But, you see, these were rather special visitors. They didn't come round for a glass of sherry and a game of 'Give Us A Clue'. They were shepherds and with them, no doubt, the first recorded Christmas present - probably a woolly jumper. And one of them, I'm sure, brought a lamb and, yet another, the roast potatoes and veg. And there it was, the first Christmas dinner.

And then came the three wise men from the east (probably Turkey). They brought gifts of gold, myrrh and frankincense. How many of you get presents like that? How many of you know what frankincense means? How many of you know why my wife buys me a tie every year? *(he fingers his dog collar)*

And so, when Christmas comes around again and you deck the halls with sprigs of holly, I want you to remember that we are celebrating the greatest of miracles - and we should be happy to do so.

After all - 'Tis the season to be jolly

Fa, la, la, la, la, la, la, la, la.'

HAPPY CHRISTMAS!

ONE-STAR HOTEL
By David Robinson

CAST:
Innkeeper

Innkeeper Number One

Innkeeper enters carrying bedding. He calls off stage to his wife.

INNKEEPER:

> All right, Esther, my love, I'll be there to help you in a matter of moments. Yes, we are going to need all the rooms making up for tonight... we have a full house, I am pleased to say.

> No room at the inn, sir. That is what I told him. The couple I mean. I hadn't seen them before, not round here. Out-of-town types, if you ask me. But I could see that they were in need of a rest, particularly her... if you know what I mean. She was very flushed in the face. The donkey didn't look too clever either.

> So anyway, I said they could have the stable around the back. Get the ox to move over a bit and they might well find a warm patch on the floor. I gave them both a towel and a bucket of water and off they went. They seemed quite grateful. I did have to say I couldn't help them with a meal... all my tables are booked well in advance this time of year.

> Oh, I also gave them a little lamp to put in the front window, just in case they got any

visitors. But to be honest, they didn't look
the type to be getting many visitors. No, I
wouldn't think so; not them.

Innkeeper calls off stage to Esther.

All right, Esther, my love... just coming.
Oh, and you can tell that complaining man in
room number sixteen that this hotel always
has been and always will be a ONE STAR
hotel. He can see it through the hole in his
roof if he looks carefully. Coming, my love.

Innkeeper exits.

Innkeeper Number Two

*Innkeeper enters carrying a reservations book. He
calls off stage to his wife.*

INNKEEPER:

All right, Esther, my love. I will be there
to help you in a matter of moments. Yes, we
will need all the tables setting for this
evening. A full house again, I am pleased to
say.

No, not a table to be had. That's what I
told the country folk who called in. I'm
pretty sure they were country folk judging
by what they brought in on their boots. Made
a dreadful mess on our new hall carpet; what
Esther will say when she sees it, I've no
idea. Mind you, they had been walking quite

a while; come down off the hills, quite a
trek. I could understand they were pretty
hungry. They were keen on me rustling up
some shepherd's pie. Nothing I could do,
tables need to be booked well in advance
this time of year.

They'd been round the back visiting the
couple with the new baby. Left them a couple
of presents; apparently a woolly jumper and
a knitted scarf. Funny sort of presents,
never catch on.

They said I ought to free up our little
function room for some special guests who
might be heading our way. One, or two or
maybe three wise types, apparently.

Innkeeper calls off stage to Esther.

All right, Esther, my love... just coming.
You can tell the complaining man in room
sixteen, there's not a lot I can do about
the piercing angelic voice outside his
bedroom window. It's probably our young
Lydia warming up for her school concert this
evening. And if she thinks dressing up in a
silk bed sheet makes her look like an opera
star, tell her it doesn't and she needs to
get it back to the linen cupboard as soon as
possible.

Coming, my love.

Innkeeper exits.

Innkeeper Number Three

Innkeeper enters carrying a high chair. He calls off stage to his wife.

INNKEEPER:

> All right, Esther, my love. I will be there to help you in a matter of moments. Yes, we will need to prepare the small function room as soon as possible; table for three and a space for the camels round the back.
>
> Finally, I am getting the class of clientele I have always wanted. I mean, we have never had American Express Gold here before. Let alone such regal figures... I rather cheekily asked if tonight meant my little hotel could now have a sign above the door... 'By Royal Appointment'. Yes, said the one in the red cloak, I certainly could have such a sign. But not because of them – because of the couple and the baby in the stable.
>
> I wasn't totally sure what he meant, but I am beginning to realise there may be a little more to this newborn baby than I first thought.
>
> So I might pop round there later, invite them in for a bit of dinner... I mean, everyone's gone so there is plenty of room, and I got this high chair down from the attic. Not been used since Lydia was tiny.
>
> Trouble is we are virtually out of food... all I can offer them are vegetables... mainly sprouts, never popular this time of year.

He seems to be attracting people from all
sides of the social scene... country
shepherds and eastern kings. Must be pretty
special.

Calls off stage to Esther.

All right, Esther, my love, just coming. The
man in room number sixteen has been round to
see what all the fuss was about... he's back
now and he's not complaining any more. Why
don't you go round, my love? It might do you
wonders... who knows, no more nagging
perhaps. Then I really will believe this is
a night of miracles. Coming, my love.

Innkeeper exits.

AND IN THAT SAME FIELD
By David Robinson

CAST:
Leonard (shepherd)
Marvin (shepherd)

LEONARD: Not really seen a star so bright before or
         since. Right up yonder, it was, as bright as
         a buckle.

MARVIN: Button.

LEONARD: One of those as well. Bright as a button –
         a row of buttons if you like. What a sight
         Marvin, what a...

MARVIN: Sight.

LEONARD: Right.

MARVIN: Bright?

LEONARD: Right and quite a sight. Talking of a bright
         light creating quite a sight, the angels did
         their bit as well. A whole great crowd of
         them there was. A heavenly toast.

MARVIN: Host.

LEONARD: That as well. Slices of 'em.

MARVIN: Toast?

LEONARD: No, host. Looked like a ghost.

MARVIN: How many?

LEONARD: Mustn't boast, a hundred at most.

MARVIN: Hundred.

LEONARD: Mustn't boast. Hundred at most, heavenly
           host looked like a ghost.

MARVIN: What about the toast?

LEONARD: Not for me, thanks. So we had to go.

MARVIN: Go?

LEONARD: Yes, we had to go go.

MARVIN: To where? Where?

LEONARD: We had to go go to Bethlehem to see the
           newborn baby lying with a stranger.

MARVIN: Don't you mean a manger?

LEONARD: Who with?

MARVIN: Well, I don't know who with.

LEONARD: You mean to tell me he was lying in a manger
           with a stranger?

MARVIN: But not in danger.

LEONARD: Not in danger with a stranger in a manger.
           Someone should fetch the ranger.

MARVIN: No danger - I said. He was with his mother.

LEONARD: Mary treasured everything we said, and
           pondered on the words.

MARVIN: What did you say to make her ponder?

LEONARD: *(he sings verse two of 'Silent Night' –
            very out of tune)*

            Silent night, holy night.
            Shepherds quake at the sight.
            Glories stream from heaven afar,
            heavenly hosts sing 'Alleluia!
            Christ, the Saviour, is born!
            Christ, the Saviour, is born!'

            All who heard the singing shepherd were
            amazed.

MARVIN: I'm not surprised.

LEONARD: And then we went home glorifying and grazing
            God.

MARVIN: Glorifying and grazing God?

LEONARD: The shepherds were glorifying – the sheep
            were grazing. And all that we saw was just
            as we had been told.

MARVIN: What a night.

LEONARD: Exactly Marvin – what a fright.

MARVIN: Night.

LEONARD: Quite, we saw a flight in the night, that
            gave us a fright, ever so bright, angels –
            polite at quite a height, and what a light.
            They said, 'Go to the baby' – we said we
            might but time was tight. 'Follow the star
            shining bright – past the chip shop and take
            a right.' So we took a right at the Friar's
            Delight, and there was the baby wrapped in
            white. And to our delight he loved the
            gifts. 'Thank you,' she said. 'Just right
            and ever so bright. A knitted pullover in

blue and white with fluffy lambs.' 'That's
right,' I said. 'Glad you like it.' 'Thank
you for coming,' she said. 'Remember the
sights and lights and frights of this
night.' And the shepherds went home and we
treasured all we had seen.

MARVIN: Quite a sight.

LEONARD: Too right. 'Remember this night,' she said,
           'the lights, sights and frights and go home
           and treasure all you have seen.'

MARVIN: Treasure - look after, a prize possession,
           keep safe, of great value - nothing trite.

LEONARD: Quite right; a wonderful, wonderful night.

Blackout.

TABLE FOR THIRTEEN

By David Robinson

CAST:
Geoff (restaurant manager)
Joyce (waitress)

Lights come up on Geoff. He is standing by a booking desk. On it is a diary and a telephone. Geoff is speaking on the telephone.

GEOFF: Yes, yes, that's right, you are speaking to the restaurant proprietor, yes. My name's... Geoff. *(pause)* Oh, hello, yes, how are you? Yes, that's right, I used to run the small fast-food place on the bypass. Yes... 'The Little Geoff', that's it. Yes, I'm running a much bigger establishment now in town - very well, thanks, yes.

Now, I'm right in thinking you are organising the conference here on 'The importance of tithing in the church - how we all should do it and there's no excuses accepted.' Yes... and you wanted to book a lunch table for all the delegates, didn't you... yes. *(making a note)* So that's a table for two, yes. Oh, I see one's dropped out, oh yes - very well. I'm sure we can squeeze you in. All right, thank you, yes - see you next week. Thank you. Bye.

Geoff now addresses the audience, whilst setting a table.

It was soon after that I got a call. A call that started the series of events. I mean,

I didn't really check what was happening
until I read about him later in the papers —
I mean, ever since then it's been quite a
useful publicity gimmick for me. Anyway,
like I said, it started with a phone call.
(phone rings) I told you.

Hello, the Pitchers of Water Restaurant and
Conference Centre — how can I help you?
(pause) Yes, oh yes, for how many? Oh,
thirteen... I'm not sure I can help you
there, sir — it's Passover, you see — oh,
you do see, yes. It is a very busy time, you
know — literally no room at the inn, sir.
Oh, you've done that story — right — yes.
Well, I could offer you the attic room. My
dear wife is intending to give it a good
cleaning up tomorrow. I mean, it's dirty, a
bit creepy, covered in cobwebs — but she's
very good with the kids. No, no, I'm joking
of course. Now, so that's the attic room, a
table for thirteen — the set Passover menu
with bread. And now, do you require water or
wine, sir? *(pause)* It's all the same to
you... I see, OK. I'll see you next week,
then — yes — 7.30. Yes, it's very easy to
find, just follow the signs with 'Pitchers
of Water' on. Thank you sir, bye-bye.

Joyce comes in.

JOYCE: Geoff, the lunch party of church treasurers
           have finished their coffee. They want to
           know if they can defer paying their bill to
           the new financial year, and any chance of
           gift-aiding their tip?

GEOFF: Not again. Tell their chairman to pop in and
           see me, could you, before he goes?

JOYCE: All right, Geoff. He's just taking up a
           collection at the moment. *(she exits)*

GEOFF: Thank you, Joyce. *(he returns to setting the
           table)* As soon as they arrived I knew there
           was something different. One of the guys –
           I thought he was the leader... but he said
           to me, 'Listen, I don't need any waiters or
           waitresses tonight. Just leave the food and
           drink outside the room – I want to serve
           them all myself.' That made me think he
           wasn't the leader. But when I quizzed him
           about it as he was leaving, he said that the
           greatest amongst us should take the lowest
           ranks. I mean, he insisted on paying for
           everyone as well as leaving a very generous
           tip for all the staff. He said he would
           certainly remember this place and was
           effusive in his compliments. I gave him one
           of my cards, of course, and said I hoped
           that would help him to remember me. Then, he
           gave me this slice of bread and drop of red
           wine in a glass. He thanked me for
           everything and said he hoped this would help
           me remember him. *(slow blackout)*

MORNING
By David Robinson

CAST:
Judas
Mary, mother of James
Simon Peter

JUDAS: *(enters somewhat agitated)*

It was early in the morning. It was very early. They said it would be. In the end it was about five-thirty, six at the latest.

There was a crowd of them. They all arrived out of the darkness, stony-faced, whispering to each other and pointing at various people. I avoided looking at them. I just couldn't look at anyone. I wanted to stop it. I honestly wanted to stop it. It was too late. It was much too late.

In the end it was quick. They grabbed him and pushed him to the ground. They bound his hands behind his back and they... they literally dragged him away.

I couldn't speak. I couldn't look at anyone else. I'd betrayed him and I knew it. I knew it meant his death. And so did he.

In the end I just ran. I ran to the temple. I went straight upstairs. I just crashed into the committee room. I said, 'There's your money. Have it back, have it back... I have betrayed innocent blood.'

You know what they said? They said, 'That's your responsibility. And now it's too late.'

I left their blood money on the floor, and I
walked out. I just walked and walked. He'll
be dead before the week's out. So will I.

Music link. Judas exits. Mary, mother of James, enters.

MARY: *(she talks in quite a hurried, almost*
             gossipy, cockney accent)

             It was early. Very early. Couldn't have been
             any later than six o'clock. I mean, yes, I
             do normally get up pretty early on a Sunday
             but, even for me, it was a bit much. It was
             Mary's idea. It would be. Mary Magdalene,
             full of good ideas that one. She saw me
             going down the supermarket last night.
             I bought a whole load of spices and oils –
             cost me a fortune.

             We arranged to meet on Sunday at six o'clock
             at the corner of my street, the three of us.
             Mary Magdalene, Salome and me. The other two
             were waiting for me when I arrived. I was
             late as usual. I can never leave the house
             in the morning without a very quick coffee.
             Bit of toast. I grabbed a banana on the way
             out. Well, you never know, do you?

             We made up the time, though. The other two
             walked at a very fast pace. I had trouble
             keeping up with 'em. I kept asking them who
             they expected to shift that huge stone from
             the front of the tomb. Well, I mean,
             I couldn't help, not with my back the way it
             is.

             When we got there, the sun was well up. It
             was quite warm for that time of day. There
             were no guards to be seen in the garden. We
             all stopped when we saw the tomb. Nobody

said a word for ages. Then Mary very slowly
and very deliberately held onto my arm.

She spoke very quietly. 'The stone... the
stone's been moved to one side.'

We all went towards the tomb, out of the
light and the heat, and into the dark and
the cold. It took me a while to adjust to
the dark. I stood just inside the tomb.
I looked all round the cave. I saw this
figure in the corner, sat on a rock. Well,
I let out a scream. I don't mind telling
you, I screamed. I was just about to leg it
out of there when he stood up. He smiled,
looked directly at us, and he spoke very
quiet and calm-like.

'Don't be afraid,' he said. 'I know who you
are looking for.'

'Yes,' I said. 'We're looking for Jesus,
Jesus the Nazarene.'

'He was here,' he said. 'But now he has
gone.'

Well I had to ask, 'Where's he gone, then?'

'He's risen,' he said. 'Now go, and please
tell the others what you have seen. Believe
me, you will see him again in Galilee.'

Well, it took us twice as long to get home.
I couldn't stop myself shaking. None of us
said a word to each other.

I mean, I saw him. I saw him crucified;
bleeding, hung on a cross, nails in his
hands, nails in his feet. I saw him. I saw
him. He was dead.

Music link comes in. Mary exits. Simon Peter enters.

SIMON PETER: *(young, excited voice)*

It was certainly early in the morning. Very
early. In fact, we'd been out there all
night. We'd missed breakfast without really
realising it. We always used to fish at
night, best time really. I loved it, I
really loved it. Just seemed the natural
thing to go back to, after... well, you
know.

Anyway, this particular morning, it was
really cold. We hadn't caught a thing, not a
single bite all night.

I said to Thomas, I said, 'Right, that's it.
Turn it round. We're going back.' I was cold
and... and I was very hungry.

'Who's that?' he said. I looked to the
shore. This bloke was standing there, ankle
deep in the water, just looking at us and
smiling. As we got nearer, he suddenly
shouted at us, 'Caught anything, my
friends?'

'No, we haven't, *my friend*,' I said. 'Got
any bright ideas?'

'Yes, yes I have,' he said. 'Try putting
your nets on the other side of your boat.'

To be honest, I was so fed up I would've
done anything. So we did it. We threw all
the nets over the side and we waited.
I thought I'd seen most things over the last
few years. I mean, it took us a good twenty
minutes to haul it all in. I have never ever
seen such a catch. I was still leaning over

the side getting the last of 'em in when I
heard John say, 'It's the Lord... Simon...
It's the Lord!'

I didn't look to check. I just grabbed my
jacket and jumped into the water. It was
freezing. I didn't care. Half swimming, half
walking, half splashing all over the place,
I just wanted to get back to the shore as
quickly as I could.

He was back, you see. He said he would be
back and now he was. He was back.

By the time I'd crawled out to the water,
he already had fish cooking on a fire.
We brought him plenty more fish. I mean,
after all that had happened, we just sat
there and watched him 'make breakfast for
us'.

He gave us bread, and then he gave us fish.
None of us asked who he was. We knew who he
was. It was the Lord. And he was back.
We didn't know for how long. It didn't
really matter. We just sat with him and had
breakfast.

Music link - Simon Peter exits.